W9-ARD-690

The World of Ancient Israel

The World of Ancient Israel

Text by
David Meilsheim (Edersheim, D)
Translated by Grace Jackman

Tudor Publishing Company
New York

Table of Contents

Library of Congress: 73-7601

1. Approaches: Galilee, Judaea and Jerusalem

Palestine is a predominantly mountainous region. In very early times the area was known as Canaan, or "lowland", because, according to Genesis X: 15-19, the Canaanites settled in the low country of Phoenicia and spread from there to the Dead Sea. The term "Palestine", or "Land of the Philistine", was first applied to the whole area at the time of the Romans. Its physical geography is probably more diverse than that of any other region of similar size in the world. Along the Mediterranean coast of Palestine a Coastal Plain. runs, without interruption, as far north as Mount Carmel, which rises like the prow of an ancient vessel in high seas. The land lying north of Mount Carmel is the Plain of St. Jean of Acre. The southern coast is divided into two parts by the hill of Joppa, with the northern part known as the Plain of Sharon, and the southern part known as the Plain of Shephelah.

Running parallel to this coast is a long range of fairly characterless, rounded mountains. Towards the north, they form the highlands of Galilee. Those to the south include the highlands of Ephraim (Samaria) and of Judah (Judaea). To the east, these hills plunge into the deep valley of El-Ghôr, the Jordan Valley. Beyond stretch the uplands of Moab and the dome of Gilead warmly coloured by the strong sunlight. Huge oak forests alternate with small plains suitable for sheep farming. This section is cleft by the Yarmuk River, which joins the Jordan a few miles below the Sea of Galilee. The northern part of the Eastern Plateau is the good farmland of Bashan. To the south of the Yarmuk Valley are the mountains of Gilead, crossed by the Jabbok River. South of Gilead, the plateau surface is very flat again, forming the Plains of Moab opposite Jericho.

Looking at the country from north to south, there are four parallel strips: the Coastal Plain, the Western Highlands, the Jordan Valley and the Eastern Plateau.

Biblical and classical authors praise the exceptional fertility of the soil.

The Bible talks of a land flowing with milk and honey. The population was proportionate to the fertility of the country. Inhabited at the time of Abraham by many peoples, it was able to provide for large herds of cattle and flocks of sheep. At the time of the census of David, there were 5 million inhabitants, roughly 10,000 per square mile. The population seems to have been even higher at the time of Christ.

Ancient books seem to have called Palestine simply "the country" and the rest of the Universe was termed "outside the country". The expression "Holy Land", so common among later generations of Jews and among Christians, is never mentioned in the Talmud. For them there was no question of comparison between Palestine and other countries. She alone was Holy.

The Mishna indicates that the glory of Palestine belongs to an area with three possible different boundaries. The smallest area covers all the territory taken by the Israelites who returned from captivity in Babylon: from Judaea to Chezib, three leagues north of Ptolemais (Acre). The second covers the territory taken by the Israelites who came up from Egypt after the Exodus: as far east as the Euphrates River and as far north as

View of a valley, taken from Mount Carmel; in the background, Haifa.

Amanah (presumably a river in Syria). The largest is defined by some ideal lines which seem to indicate what the country should have been according to the original promise of God, although Israel never spread its dominion that far.

On the border of the territory around that inhabited by the Jews, there was a dense circle of nations that practised idolatrous rites, customs and religion.

The Jews who returned from Babylon after the exile were comparatively few in number. They did not, as we have said, occupy all of the country that they had occupied prior to the exile. During the troubled period following their delivrance, there was a constant immigration of pagans, and unceasing attempts were made to introduce and keep in the Holy Land those foreign elements which had become intermingled with the legitimate descendents of the fathers of Israel. The very language of the Jews had changed considerably. Over the centuries, ancient Hebrew had been completely replaced by the Aramaean dialect except in public worship and in the learned academies of the theologians.

When the Jews returned from the Babylonian exile, the north-easternmost part of Palestine (the territory which would eventually be governed by the tetrarch Philip and which had once been part of Manasseh's possession) was populated with scarcely civilized peoples who were given to thieving. Most of them lived in the huge grottos in which they accumulated their provisions. When they were attacked, they would defend themselves and their herds, which were their main wealth, to the death. Herod the Great and his successors subjugated these peoples and had many Jews and Idumaeans settle among them. (The Idumaens, who had also been in exile in Babylon, were first led to the area by a certain chief Zamaris.) Like some of the German immigrants in parts of Russia, they were attracted by the tax exemption. But most of the population continued to be made up of uncouth, barbarous Syrians and Greeks.

"If a man seeks wealth, let him go to the north; if he seeks knowledge, let him come to the south of Palestine". This was the axiom that the priests liked to repeat to make the distinction between the material riches of Galilee, and the higher knowledge of Tradition which they claimed for Judaea as such. Unfortunately, it was not long before Judaea was stripped of this dubious grandeur. The academies were forced to go north and ended up near Lake Genesareth (the sea of Galilee) in the town of Tiberias.

But as long as Jerusalem and Judaea were the centre of Jewish instruction, no expression of scorn was too strong to express the condescension with which a Rabbinist, a zealous observer of the rules of the law, regarded his co-religionnists living in the north. The insulting question of Nathanael: "Can there any good thing come out of Nazareth?" was a by-word of the time, and the reprimand of the Pharisees to Nicodemus: "Art thou also of Galilee? Search and look: for out of Galilee arises no prophet." Here is more than awareness of superiority on the part of the town population, as those of Jerusalem were known, *vis-à-vis* their country cousins. It was an offensive remark, scorn expressed

The River Jordan (at the spot where by tradition Christ was baptised).

without any refinement, but always with a deep feeling of the dignity of the person delivering the insult.

Impartial history, however, holds a different view of the inhabitants of Galilee from that of the priesthood. The province covered the territory of four tribes, Issachar, Zebulun, Naphtali and Asher. It was bordered on the south by Samaria and on the west by Mount Carmel. Its border to the east was the district of Scythopolis (in the Decapolis). On this side, the Jordan and Lake Genesareth formed a general frontier. In Galilee are several places of historical importance. Here are the mountains of Gilboa, eternal witnesses of the defeat of Israel and Saul, small Mount Hermon, Mount Tabor, Mount Carmel and the greatest battlefield in Palestine, the Valley of Jezreel. The Talmud and Josephus divide it into upper and lower Galilee separated by the district of Tiberias, regarded as middle Galilee. Safed was a city built on a height. Kefr-Anan, to the north-west of Safed, is mentioned as the main city of upper Galilee. The Talmud calls it by the name of Zephath. It was one of the outposts from which the signal of the new moon could be transmitted. This signal, given by the Sanhedrin in the city of Jerusalem, marked the beginning of each month. Beacon fires sent the signal to every town throughout the country and, far to the east, to the Jews living among the Gentiles, with the signal being transmitted from mountain to mountain.

In the mountainous part of upper Galilee the scenery was wonderful. The air vivified the whole body. Here one part of the drama of the Song of Solomon was played out. But its grottos and fortresses and marshy land were also a refuge for wrong-doers, outlaws and leaders of revolt. Going deeper into the heart of this province, the countryside changed completely. South of Lake Merom, where what is known as Jacob's Bridge crosses the Jordan, we come to the large caravan route that linked Damascus on the east to the big market of the town of Ptolemais on the Mediterranean coast. It facilitated innumerable commercial enterprises, and it is easy to imagine how many pairs of hands were kept busy by this incessant traffic. All day long, streams of camels, mules and donkeys passed this way laden with the riches of the east, heading for the far-off countries of the west, or bringing the wealth of western countries to the furthermost regions of the Levant. Travellers of every nationality—Jews, Greeks, Romans who lived in eastern countries journeyed together on these interminable convoys. These continual relations with foreigners, the passage of all these different peoples, made it almost impossible for Galilee to be as bigoted as Judaea.

It is hard to imagine a more beautiful and more fertile region than Galilee. This indeed was the country where Asher should dip his foot in oil, in the words of Deuteronomy. The oil of the country, we are told, ran like a river, and it was said that is was easier to cultivate a forest of olive trees in Galilee than to raise a single child in Judaea. Wine, although less abundant, flowed free and strong. Grain grew on the spreading plains, particularly around Capernaum. Flax was also grown. The cost of living was much lower than in Judaea, where one measure was

These imposing desert hills lie between Jericho and the Jordan. Left: a view of Galilee, near Nazareth.

said to cost as much as five in Galilee. As for fruit, it was excellent.

Josephus describes the country in really enthusiastic terms. There were no less than 240 towns or villages and the smallest of these numbered at least 15,000 inhabitants. This is a gross exaggeration, but it is true that commercial life was intense. There were also diverse industries, various potteries and dyeworks. From the heights of Galilee, you could see ports filled with trading vessels. At the traveller's feet lay a sea of azure billowing with sails. The trunk route that crossed the province went through Capernaum, down to Nazareth and followed the coast. The rabbinical books tell us that Nazareth was one of the halts of the Jewish priests. These were divided into two classes, one always employed in the levitical duties in the temple. By a significant coincidence then, this city was traversed by both those men whose lives were given over to trade and the material things of this world, and those whose existence was spent in the shade of the altars of Jehovah.

In the north lay the large town of Caphernaum. Near by lay Chorazin, whose wheat was so renowned that, if this town had been closer to Jerusalem, it could have been used for the temple. Then came Bethsaida, whose name "house of fishing", denotes its usual trade.

South of Caphernaum lies Magdala, the town of dyers. The Talmud mentions its shops, woollen materials, great wealth and also the corruption of its inhabitants. Tiberias, which had been founded shortly before the coming of Christ, is mentioned in passing

Ancient Jewish potteries.

Below: the ruins of the synagogue of Capernaum.

in the New Testament. It was a town with magnificent buildings forming a striking contrast with the more modest dwellings of the inhabitants.

The writings of the great Jewish sages show up certain differences which, morally speaking, separated the Jews of Galilee from those of Judaea. We cannot go into them here, but we can without hesitation say that the first showed more practical sincere piety, more rigour in their life, and less slavish attention to the Pharisaic distinctions which robbed the law of its very essence. On the other hand, the Talmud accuses the Galileans of neglecting tradition and of joining the school of one scholar one day and another the day after (perhaps because they had for teachers only visiting rabbis and not an established academy). It regards them as incapable of reaching the height of the distinctions and subtle explanations of Rabbinism. Josephus tells us that their hot blood made them quick to anger.

Their poor pronunciation of Hebrew, or rather their lack of ability to enunciate the gutturals, was a constant topic of raillery and bitter reproach on the part of all classes of inhabitants of Judaea. Josephus describes the Galileans as solid workers and brave men. The Talmud says they cared more for honour than for money.

The part of the province easiest to conjure up is that around the lake. Its beauty, wonderful vegetation, almost tropical products, its wealth, and considerable population have often been described. According to the scriptures, the name Genesareth is taken from "a harp", because the fruits of the lake side

The banks of Lake Genesareth. In the background Mount Hermon. ("The name Genesareth comes from a harp because the fruits of the banks of this lake were as sweet as the sound of this instrument").

were as sweet as the sound of one. It is also sometimes said to mean "garden of princes", because of the beautiful towns and the green gardens surrounding it.

Galilee could well be proud of the beauty of its countryside or the fertility of its plains. It could rightly claim to be a market where there was extremely lively activity. It was also a mediator, bringing Israel closer to the ancient world which lay outside the limits of Palestine. Judaea, on the contrary, did not envy any one of these attributes. Its legitimate source of pride was quite different. If Galilee was the outer courtyard of the temple, Judaea was the very sanctuary of Israel. It is true that it had only arid landscape to offer, bare rocky hills and lonely deserts. But the events of sacred history, the religious dramas of the nation of Israel had taken place in the shade of its stark mountains. When the pilgrim turned his back on the rich, luxuriant plains of Galilee, he literally went up to Jerusalem. The eternal hills rose before him, in ever heightened majesty, until on the summit above them, he saw the sanctuary of God, eclipsing by its magnificance the beauty of the surrounding scenery, appear to his enchanted eyes in its bright robe of marble and gold. As the mingled noises of life gradually faded from his ears as he went into the solitary silence surrounding Zion, the well-known places he passed through seemed to awake before him the echoes of the history of his people.

Here he comes to Shiloh, the oldest sanctuary of Israel, where, according to tradition, the ark remained 370 years. Or Bethel, with its sacred memories of the time of the patriarchs. Here the angel of death had been stripped of his power. Now he reaches the plateau of Ramal and the neighbouring highlands of Gibeon and Gibeah, scene of great events in the history of God's people. It was at Ramah that Rachel died and was buried. We know that Jacob erected a column on her tomb. Erected five miles from Jerusalem, this column must have been a well known milestone. On the other side of the valley the tombs of Bilhah and Dinah were dug. Near this memorial of the sad, dishonoured days of Jacob, the captive Jews were herded together before being led to Babylon.

To the west, the mountains fall away abruptly towards Shephelah or the Coastal Plain. Here, Joshua pursued the kings of the south and Samson hurled himself upon the Philistines. Here, for many a long year, war was waged against the hordes of the Philistines, implacable enemies of Israel. Going further south, beyond the capital lies royal Bethlehem, and further on, the city of the priests, Hebron, with its grottos full of the most precious remains of Israel. The Desert of Judaea is a highland plateau that was known by different names in the various villages scattered in lonely places, sometimes inhabited by a single shepherd or a large landowner. This desert had long been the haunt of those who set themselves against society, or the refuge of solitary wanderers who, disgusted with the world, lived as recluses. It was in these grottos hollowed in the flank of the calcinated rock that David and his men hid. It was here that many bands of partisans had often found refuge. Here again the Essenes had hid in the vain hope of finding purity

by cutting themselves off from the society of men. Further on, in the mysterious depths of the horizon, like an immobile plain, lay the Dead Sea, a perpetual memorial to the judgement of God. On the west bank rose the castle to which Herod had given his name, and further south was the almost inaccessible fortress of Masada, scene of the last act of the great tragedy in the terrible war of Judaea.

A few hours journey from the desolate banks of the Dead Sea, the traveller came upon a kind of earthly paradise. Flanked and defended by four forts on all sides, the town of Jericho stood tall and proud. Herod had built its walls, its theatres, its amphitheatres; Archelaus had erected its new palace surrounded by splendid gardens. Pilgrims travelling from Galilee passed through Jericho. It was also on the main caravan route linking Arabia to Damascus. The fertility of its land and its fruits were of particularly high renown. Its palm-tree groves, rose gardens, and particularly the plantations of balm, the most extensive of which lay behind the royal garden, made this fairyland.

Here was the deep depression of Arabah, into which flowed the waters of the Jordan. The river rushed impetuously on until it neared the Dead Sea, where it ran slowly, as if to show the repugnance the sacred river felt at entering these muddy waters. Pilgrims, priests, traders, thieves, anchorites, and fanatics played their part on this strange stage and at the same time there seemed to be heard in the distance the holy chanting of the divine worship celebrated on Mount Zion in the temple of Jehovah.

The historians, with reference to Judaea, say that no one would have run the risk of undertaking a difficult was to conquer the country. For the Israelite, however, this was the refuge of his soul, the centre of his interior life, the desire of his heart: "If I forget thee, O Jerusalem, let my right hand forget her cunning". Thus sang the captives of Jacob as they sat near the rivers of Babylon weeping at the memory of Zion. "If I do not remember thee, let my tongue cleave to the roof of my mouth; if I prefer not Jerusalem above my chief joy".

The sounds of the pilgrims reached their greatest intensity when the city of their hopes lay for the first time before their eyes: "For the LORD hath chosen Zion; he hath desired it for his habitation. This is my rest for ever; here will I dwell; for I have desired it. I will abundantly bless her provision: I will satisfy her poor with bread. I will also clothe her priests with salvation: and her saints shall shout aloud for joy. There I will make the horn of David to bud: I have ordained a lamp for mine anointed. His enemies will I clothe with shame: but upon himself shall his crown flourish".

Words that have been proved absolutely true in their literal and spiritual application; sublime hope for nearly 2,000 years which still forms part of the daily prayer of Israel.

For the exiles, Jerusalem was the only fold. To go, were it only once, within the sacred walls, to mingle with the worshippers, bring gifts, see the crowd of priests exercising their ministry, dressed in their white robes; to hear the chant of the Levites, see the smoke rising from the burnt offerings towards the sky—this for a son of Abraham was to fulfil the dearest dream of his life, this was heaven on earth, the certain guarantee of the fulfilment of the most wonderful promises of the ancient prophets.

The famous site of Masada, seen from the west.

Left: view of the dunes near the Dead Sea. —Opposite: portrait of Josephus Flavius born in the year 37: he is the greatest Jewish historian of Antiquity.

Below: staircase at Hebron, leading to the tombs of Abraham, Isaac and Jacob.

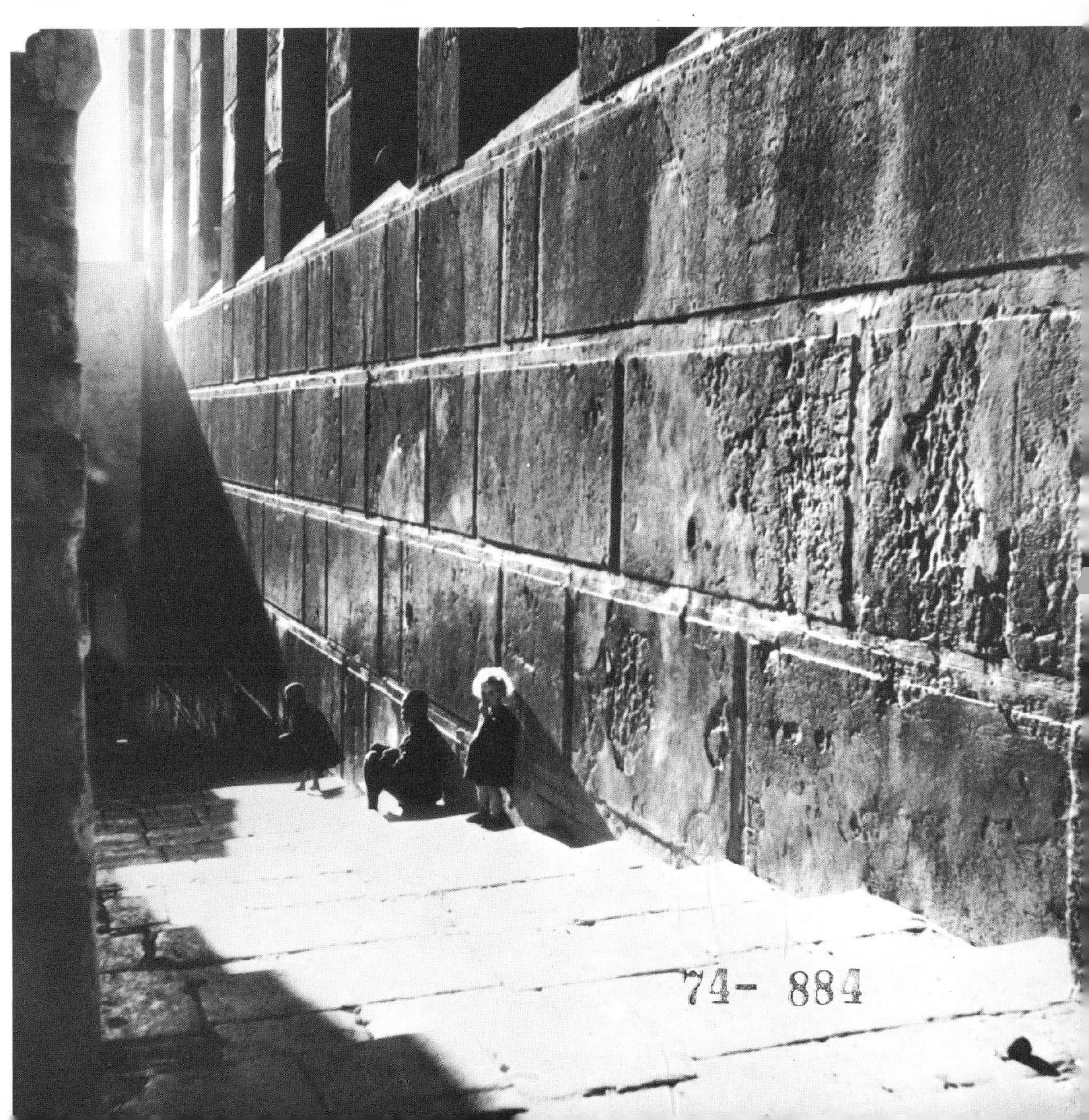

No wonder, then, that at the time of important feast days and holidays, the population of Jerusalem and its environs reaching to the holy limits of the city rose to hundreds and hundreds of thousand of people.

The priesthood reproached Galilee its language, its customs, its negligence of regular study. Certain legal observances and social customs were different in Judaea and Galilee. It was only in Judaea that the rabbis could be consecrated by the laying-on of hands. Here, the Sanhedrin in a solemn session proclaimed the beginning of every month on which depended the order of the feast days in the calendar. Even when the strict necessities of politics forced the scholars to take refuge in Galilee, they came to Lydda to make this proclamation.

The wine used in the Temple was harvested exclusively in Judaea not only because it was of higher quality, but because transport through Samaria would have sullied it. The Mishna even mentions the names of the five towns that enjoyed the privilege of providing it. The oil used in the House of the Eternal was also harvested in Judaea. The olives were brought to Jerusalem to be made into holy oil.

Which cities were really Jewish? This was a very important question because of the rituals. It received the closest attention of the leaders of Israel. It is not easy to fix the exact limits of Judaea as such on the north-west side. To include the Coastal Plain within the province of Samaria is a common error. It will never be regarded as such. According to Josephus, Judaea properly speaking spread along the banks of the Mediterranian as far north as Ptolemais, but the Talmud seems to leave out the towns in the north. It was decided that Caesarea belonged to Judaea but that its port could not enjoy the privileges granted to this province, since the country to the east and north was regarded as unclean.

To the south of Caesarea, lay the beautiful, rich Plain of Sharon. It stretched to Lydda where it merged with that of Darom, which ran further south. The Plain of Sharon was always renowned for its pastures; according to the Talmud, this was the province which provided most of the calves for sacrifice. Its wine was famous and was supposed to be drunk mixed with one-third of water. The Plain was also known for its potteries, but this must however have been of rather inferior quality. The clay used to build the brick houses was so bad that these dwellings had to be rebuilt every seven years. Hence the prayer made by the High Priest on the day of atonement in which he asked Jehovah that the houses of the inhabitants of Sharon should not become their tombs. God gave the world ten measures of beauty and nine of them were bestowed on Jerusalem, we are told. It was a city known throughout the world. In contrast with Alexandria which was called "small", the city of David was called "great". The name "Eternal City", given to Rome, springs to mind when we hear the priests talk of Jerusalem as the eternal home. A proverb says that all roads lead to Rome, but a Jewish dictum also said that all monies came from Jerusalem.

The details we are given regarding the hospitality of the inhabitants of the city of David have not been exaggerated, since it was

Remains of the walls of Jericho.

Left, old press at Capernaum. Below, sculpture (also at Capernaum) symbolising the manna received by the Hebrews in the desert.

deemed to belong to no tribe in particular. It was considered the common home for all the children of Abraham. Its houses could not be rented; they were free to all brothers. No traveller among the thousands filling the city on feast days could be without a roof over his head. A curtain was hung in front of a house to show there was still room for a guest. A table placed outside showed that the traveller was welcome at the family's table.

Every care was taken to make Jerusalem a delightful city. Its rules and regulations of health and hygiene were better than in any other city. The rules observed were such that pilgrims could freely apply their hearts and spirits, to the austere meditation that had called them to the place. If the inhabitants of the city had the reputation of being somewhat proud and disdainful, it must be admitted that they did have some reason to be. It was no small matter to be a citizen of Jerushalaimah, as they liked to write the name of their great city.

Through their constant relations with foreigners, they acquired a wide knowledge of men and the world. The vivacity and kindness of all young people was a continual topic of admiration for their more timid or more backward country cousins. They had a certain something in their behaviour that spoke oi dignity, a certain richness in their clothes and delicacy and gallantry in their manners that showed in their every action. In the midst of a people whose spirit and ability were proverbial, it is no mean praise to be known

The western wall at Jerusalem.
Digs in the Jewish district of the old town: these remains date from 700 B.C.

for these very qualities. Jerusalem was in a word the ideal city for the Jew, whatever the country of his exile.

People of means were generous with their money for the upkeep of the Jewish academies, contributing to the advancement of piety or supporting the national cause. Thus one individual, seeing that the price of sacrifices was very high, felt impelled to have all the animals needed for slaughter driven into the courtyards of the temple at his own expense, so that the poor could present the required offerings to Jehovah. Another time, during the struggle with Rome, he offered to give the town the essential provisions for 21 months.

The streets of Jerusalem were filled with men from the most far-flung corners of the earth, speaking in every tongue imaginable; Jews and Greeks, Roman soldiers and Galilean peasants, Pharisees, Sadducees, Essenes dressed in their white robes, bustling merchants, students absorbed in their abstruse theological niceties were part of the strange crowd that milled in the narrow streets of the town of palaces.

But towering above all the buildings was the Temple, dominating the city, bathing it in sacred shade and reflected glory. Every morning the three trumpet calls of the priests woke the inhabitants, inviting them to prayer; every evening, the same call of the sacred instruments ended the day. It was like a voice from heaven, inviting the tired and weary to rest. Wherever you looked, there were holy buildings veiled in the smoke from sacrifices drifting over the courtyards, wrapped in silence that seemed to have come down to the doors of the house of Jehovah from heaven. This sanctuary gave Jerusalem a special character and decided the destiny of the city.

Tree of live: *Carved in stone in part of a steps in the old town of Safad.*

On the grandiose troubled site of the mountains around Massada, a camp for the archaelogists and their co-workers.
Path leading to the ruins of Massada.

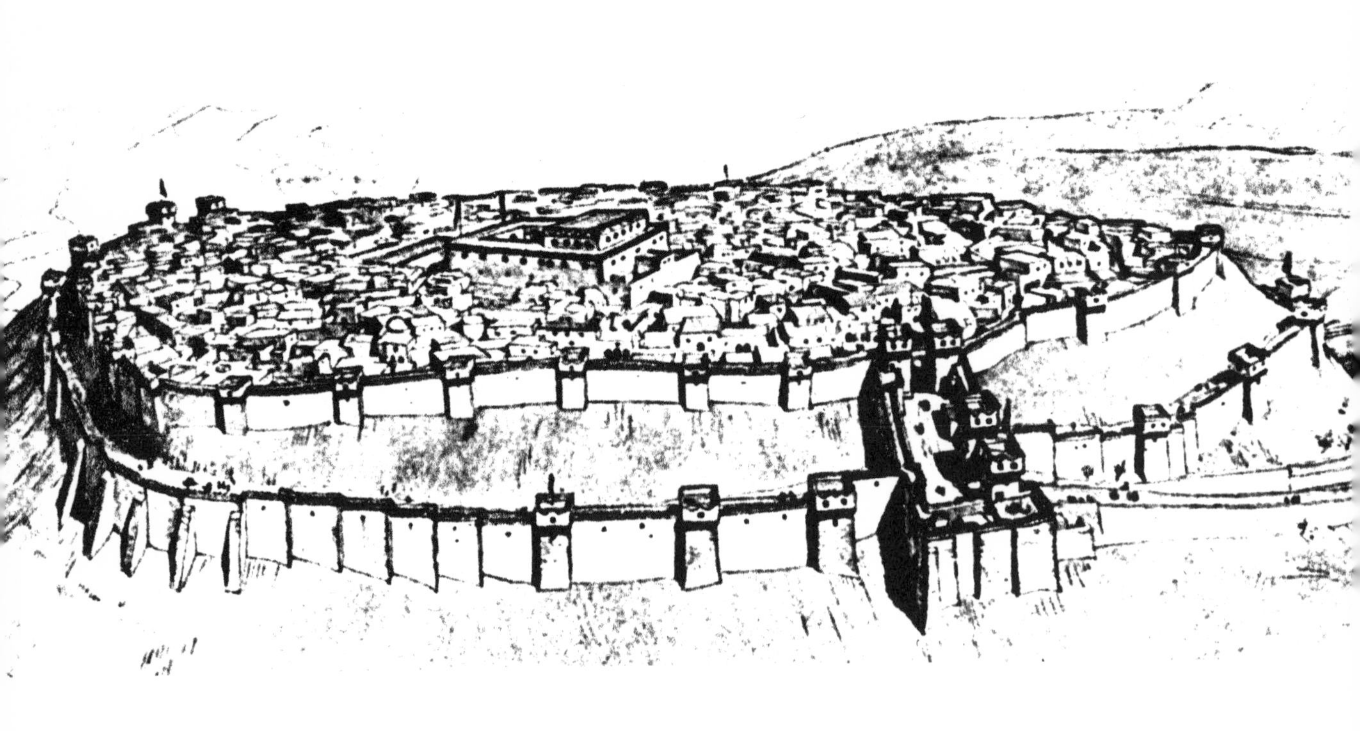

Below: reconstitution of a city, Lakish.

Above, the plateau of Massada. In the background, the Dead Sea. Below and right, two views of the site.
An expedition, lead by Professor Yigael Yadin, revealed the riches of the citadel, which served as a refuge of the last members of the Jewish resistance in the struggle against rhe Romans, and the Palace of Herod.

General view of the shops in Massada. Above, mosaic of a building in the middle of the fortress.

32

Fragment of a bas-relief of High Antiquity on the deportation of the Jews shows the wall of a Jewish city. "Most cities were built on hills and surrounded by walls."

2. The Jewish Year, Architecture, Law

The ancient Jewish calendar (still used by Jews today) was based on a year of twelve lunar months, or 354 days, with a thirteenth month of 11 days added every two or three years. This intercalary month, called Veadar or Second Adar, adjusted the months to the seasons and enabled annual festivals to occur during the same season every year.

The ancient Jews were an essentially agricultural people. The harvest legally began on the second day of Passover, or the sixteenth day of the month of Nisan (corresponding to late March or early April). It lasted about seven weeks and normally had to be finished by Pentecost. Barley was harvested first, since it was often ready by the end of March, then wheat and finally oats. The harvest was an occasion of great rejoicing; happy songs rang out on all sides. The sheaves were tied and stacked. The grain was threshed in the field and it was stored in holes in the ground. The harvesters did not pick up ears of grain that they dropped, and the law authorized the poor to come and glean (Leviticus XIX, 9; Ruth II, 2). People had the right, even when the harvest was still standing, to come and take a handful of grain, and the watchman responsible for guarding the field from damage by birds or thieves had no right to intervene.

Despite the importance of the agricultural segment of the society, the towns and cities had a prominent place in the life of the country. Most towns were built on hills and were surrounded by very thick walls. Within the walls both public buildings and private houses could usually be found.

Deuteronomy gives us some information about the construction of private houses that shows fairly advanced ideas: "When thou buildest a new house, then thou shalt make a battlement for thy roof, that thou bring not blood upon thine house, if any man fall from thence" (Deut. XXII 8).

The remarkable skill and knowledge of the ancient Jewish architects is especially evident from what is known about the construction of the Temple and of Solomon's palace.

The book of Kings tells us that Solomon ordered large and rare stones to be quarried for the foundations of the temple and that he had these stones cut with care. The historian Josephus supplements this information with the most curious details of the way in which the hill of Moriah was flattened, consolidated and transformed in order to serve as a foundation for the building: A rocky hill that was difficult to climb lay in the eastern region of the city; King Solomon, driven by divine inspiration, had a magnificant wall built around the summit of this hill. He covered the flank of the hill with enormous blocks held together with lead. The size of these blocks can be judged by seeing the surface area of the structure, the interior of which, held together by iron reinforcements, made up an absolutely indestructible mass on which time could make no impression. Josephus adds that this work had been executed at the very top of the hill and so the peak was slightly levelled. The irregularities in the surface falling within the huge enclosure wall were filled in; all rough surfaces of the rock were smoothed, so that this enclosure finally became a perfectly flat platform. This great enclosure had four stadia. Inside, the top of the hill was surrounded by another wall against which, towards the east, was a double arch as long as the wall itself, facing the entrance of the temple, which was in the middle of this enclosure. (This arch was of much later construction than the temple.) The awesome platform into which the hill of Moriah was transformed by this wonderful work has remained intact to the present time; part of the wall of the enclosure built by Solomon has withstood the successive attacks on the holy city. Some of the blocks forming the base are as much as 9 metres long and 1 metre high. No such wall was ever built by the Greeks or the Romans.

A bridge of gigantic proportions connected the temple enclosure to a square in the city, passing over Tyropeon (Valley of the Cheese-makers).

The temple was 60 cubits (125 feet) long and 20 cubits (32 1/2 feet) wide; it was 30 cubits (50 feet) high and its foundations were as deep. The pronaos or porcha in front of the temple, was 20 cubits wide and 10 cubits deep below ground and 60 cubits high above ground. The temple proper was divided length-wise into two parts, the furthest and smallest part measured 20 cubits and was the impenetrable sanctuary, the Holy of Holies. This sanctum was only 20 cubits high, while the main nave, the naos, was 30 cubits high. It is well to remember that this diminishing height was the rule in Egyptian architecture.

Josephus tells us that Solomon had three floors of rooms or aedicules built around the Temple, backing on to it; these rooms, thirty on each floor, were about 5 cubits long and

A wall of the fortress of Massada.

5 cubits wide; they were communicating rooms. Winding staircases, built into the thick walls and leading on the outside to the flanks of the building, led up to the various floors. An upper gallery, 5 cubits high (8 feet) ran around the whole body of the Temple; it was covered on the inside by cedar wood.

The internal decoration of the Temple was magnificent. Cedar wood panels hid the stone. In the Holy of Holies, these wooden walls were themselves covered with gold set with precious stones; the floor, of cypress wood, was also covered with gold to the threshold. The naos was almost as luxuriously decorated according to Josephus, who says that Solomon did not leave a single part of the temple uncovered with gold; but here it is reasonable to suppose that the historian is guilty of exaggeration. What he has to say about the materials used for the building of the Temple is, however, borne out by the information given in the Bible, and by the remains of the construction itself. The whole Temple was built, with infinite artistry, of polished blocks held together by smooth-fitting joints so that there remained no visible trace of a hammer or any other tool, and the onlooker was tempted to believe that this whole mass was assembled without man-power and endowed with spontaneous cohesion, rather than put together by human industry. The astonishing feat of construction took seven years (from 1016 to 1009 B.C.). It is true that David had gathered together a good part of the materials. Sixty thousand workers took part in the building.

Nature as troubled as the destiny of the chosen people.

The palace that Solomon had built on Mount Zion and linked to the temple by the

Reconstitution, according to historical data, of the Temple of Jerusalem and the Palace of Solomon.

bridge already mentioned testifies to the magnificence of this king of the Jews. It was built of freestone, hewn with care and covered with a facing of precious marble. A double portico, one of whose doorways gave on to a huge hall where the king dispensed justice, formed the entranceway. Other buildings, intended for feasts and festivals, had doorways that led to the monarch's chambers. Gold and precious stones gleamed everywhere.

A few more details about the Temple. It included: the Court of the Gentiles, where even strangers were admitted; the Court of the Jews, reserved for Israelites and where the sacrificial altar was; the Court of the Priests, where only Levites were admitted; then came the Holy of Holies, where only the High Priest could go once a year, on Yom Kippur.

The vases, tables, candelabra, receptacles of every kind were of gold. The main sacred objects used in the Temple were the seven-branched candelabrum of gold; the table of the shewbread; the altar of incense; the sacrificial altar; the "molten sea" of brass, a huge basin of brass, resting on twelve oxen of the same metal, that was used for the purification of the Levites; the Ark of the Covenant; a coffer containing the tables of the law; Aaron's rod; the urn of manna; and various vessels.

The priest Simeon son of Galamiel, speaking in the name of the priest-Simeon son of Sagan (assistant to the High Priest), said that the veil of the Holy of Holies was as thick as a hand's breadth. It was made of sixty-two tresses intermingled. Each tress was made of twenty-four threads (according to the Talmud, six threads of each of the four colours of the Temple, white, scarlet, blue and gold). It was 40 cubits long and 20 cubits wide. Every year, two such veils were made and 300 priests were needed to immerse them before they could be hung in the sanctuary.

The Temple of Jerusalem was pillaged under Roboam by Sesac, king of Egypt; closed by Ahab, king of Israel; changed by Manasseh, until his conversion, into a place of idolatry and superstition; finally sacked and pillaged by Nabuchodnosor when he took Jerusalem (565 B.C.). Cyrus allowed the Jews to rebuild their city and their temple (536). This more or less faithful restoration of the original was completed in the year 515. This Second Temple, pillaged by Antiochus (171) then by Crassus (54 B.C.) was rebuilt by Herod and finally ruined beyond repair and reduced to ashes by Titus, when Jerusalem was taken by Vespasian.

We are told in Numbers (VII, 84) that the princes of Israel dedicated to the altar, on the day when it was annointed, twelve chargers of silver each weighing 130 shekels; twelve silver bowls each weighing 70 shekels; and twelve spoons of gold each weighing 10 shekels. In chapter X, there are two trumpets of silver mentioned that Moses ordered to be made so that they could, if need be, serve to call the nation together and sound the alarm for departure. Later (XXI, 9) we learn that the Hebrews had camped in a region crawling with very dangerous snakes, that might well have been the basilic, royal insignia par excellence of the Egyptians, and thus Moses had a serpent of brass made so that if a serpent had bitten

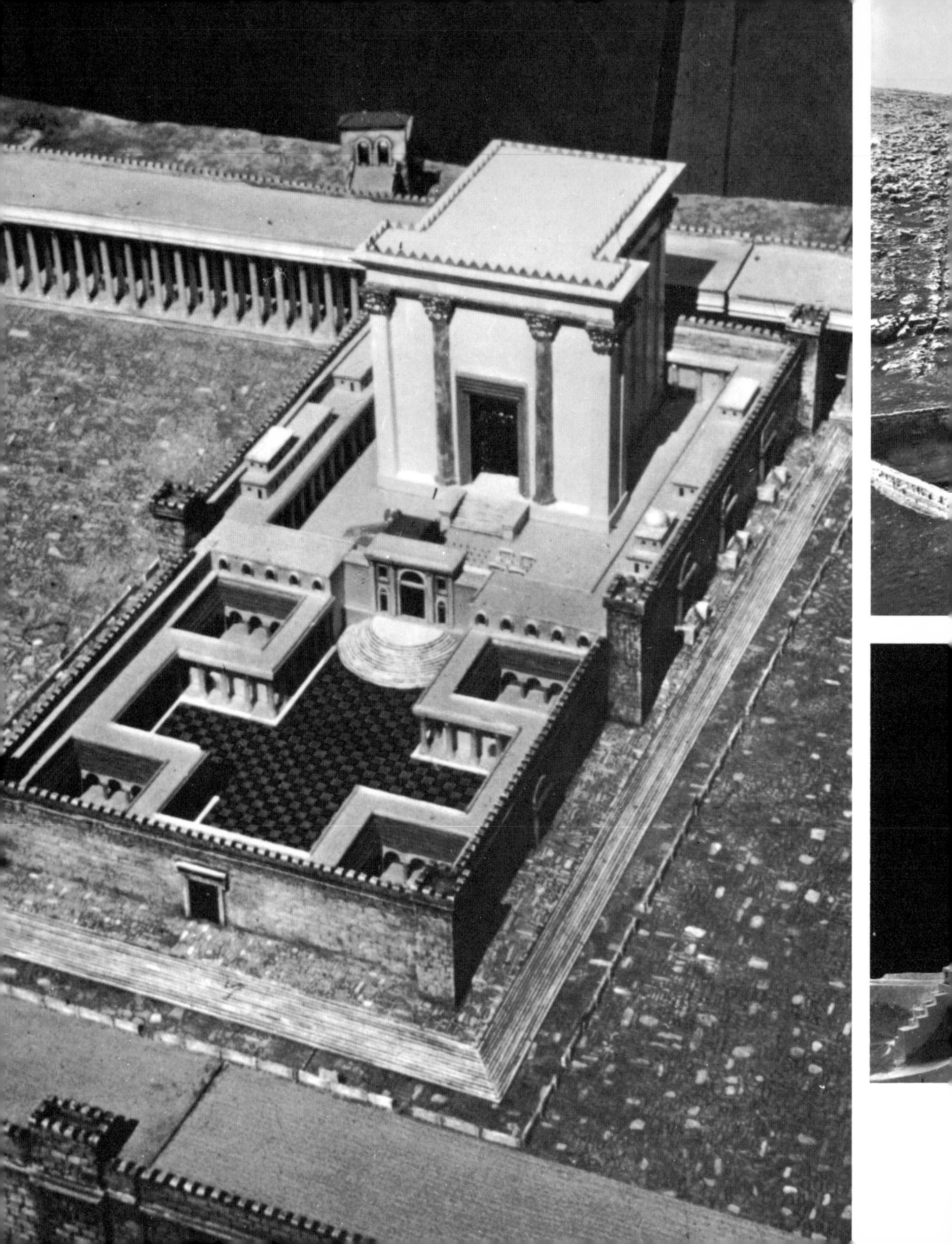

Mount Sinai. Moses showing the Torah, according to a fresco of the synagogue of Dours-Europos in Mesopotamia (circa 200 A.D.).

3. The Jewish City

The differences that separated the Jews and Gentiles were noticeable not only in the matter of religion, but in social life as well. However close the pagan towns were to those of Israel, however frequent or close the relationships between them, no one could go into an Israelite town or village without feeling they were in a new world. The look of the streets, the buildings, the way the houses were arranged, the municipal and religious rules, the manners and customs of the people, above all family life, showed a marked contrast between the Gentiles and the chosen people. One idea gradually became a conviction. Here religion was not the statement of a simple credo, nor a set of observances. It permeated every relationship of a man with those around him, directed his steps in every period of his existence.

Let us look at a really Jewish town or village. There were many. At all times, Palestine had had a great many more than might have been expected from the size of the country, or from the fact that a considerable part of its population was given over to agriculture. When Joshua's armies were taking possession of this country, there were about 600 towns. From the size of the Levite cities, it seems that most towns had a circumference of roughly 2,000 cubits and an average population of 2,000 to 3,000 people. But the number of towns and villages and their inhabitants increased remarkably in the next period. Josephus tells us, for example, that in his time there were at least 240 cities in Galilee alone. He employs three terms to describe cities; these

Coat of Arms of the State of Israel, graven on the wall of an ancient palace in Jerusalem 2200 years ago. The candlestick ("Menorah" in Hebrew) was the most precious object of the cult.

terms can best be translated as "village", "commune" and "town". All towns were distinguished by the fact that they were surrounded by walls. Many cities were already fortified at the time of Joshua; others have fortifications of much more recent date. A commune was "large" when it had a synagogue and small when it did not. There was a synagogue if the commune residents included at least ten men, the quorum for worship in the synagogue (Minyan). Religious services could not be held if there were not that number. Villages did not have synagogues. It was thought that their inhabitants would go to the market in the nearest commune on the Monday and Thursday of each week. A religious service was held for them and the local Sanhedrin met for them. One law stated that a man could not require his wife to follow him if he moved from a village to a town or vice versa. The first of these prescriptions was based on the idea that, in a town, the population lived closer together in a smaller space and houses were nearer each other. Hence there was a lack fresh air and of gardens that could be enjoyed when living in a smaller place. However, a woman could also refuse to leave a town for a village, since in towns everything needed was at hand and the inhabitants of the surrounding neighbourhood came from all sides into the streets and to the markets to bring their goods.

When a traveller approached one of the fortified cities of Palestine, he came upon a fairly low wall, protected by a ditch. After passing through, he reached the walls of the town per se. He entered the town through a massive door, often covered with iron, and fortified by thick bars and solid bolts. Above the door was a watch-tower. Once inside you stood in an empty space, shaded or sheltered, where the elders were sitting. Here serious citizens discussed public affairs, gathered the news of the day, or concluded important transactions. Large squares on which converged various roads were the scene of these lively, personal and business gatherings. The country population stood in these squares, or crossed them crying their wares, products of the field, the vineyard or the dairy. Foreign traders or bagmen showed their merchandise. They attracted passers-by by boasting of the latest fashion in Rome or Alexandria, the advantages of the most recent inventions of the wealth of the East, the artistic products of the jeweller or designer of Jerusalem. The lazy or busy crowd passed before them chattering, bargaining for the objects laid out on the tables, exchanging subtle jokes. Suddenly it would give way respectfully to a Pharisee. Conversation would stop because an Essene or a member of some religious or political sect had just appeared.

The streets all had particular names. They were mostly taken from the trade or association of traders who had set up their stalls there. Those who plied the same trade were always grouped in a special district. All the Israelites felt a kind of brotherhood, and there was even a sort of freemasonry in the way they greeted each other, which stemmed either from a recognition of the God of Israel, or a brotherly wish for peace and happiness. Quick to anger,

Groove for rain water in the ruins of a paved street of Subeita.

lively, imaginative and astute, great lovers of parables, strong sentences, subtle distinctions, amusing and epigrammatic maxims, they were full of reverence for God and men, respectful towards the aged, enthusiastic about knowledge and the superior gifts of intelligence. Extremely sensitive, fervent, quite often prejudiced, all these characters with raging passions that were as quickly cooled, made up the crowd moving around these public places.

Do you hear the voice of the priest teaching in a quiet corner under the shade of the tall trees? His listeners forget the demands of hunger and fleeting time until the day draws to a close and the stars appearing in the blue sky remind more than one of them of the promises made to their father Abraham.

Behind the town, when night falls, there is another crowd, those without cisterns in their homes, who gather around the spring or the fountain, taking pleasure in its gentle murmur. The guard is already mounted at the top of the tower, above the gate of the town, and the night-watchmen are ready to go their rounds in closed ranks. The town is not absolutely dark, because it is customary to keep a lamp burning in each house throughout the night, and the windows open mainly on to the road or on to the street.

The broader are known as Tyrian; the smaller windows are not glazed, but have gratings or bars. In elegant houses, the window-frame curves artistically, richly inlaid. The wood commonly used is sycamore, sometimes olive or cedar, and in the palaces, sandalwood that comes from India. The coping, generally curved inward, had

Foundations of the town of Meggido, built by Solomon (Xth century B.C.).

interesting or bizarre decorations. But it is forbidden to represent any object which exists in heaven or on earth. Feeling on this point was so unanimous that the attempt made by Pilate to introduce into Jerusalem, by night, effigies of Caesar mounted on standards caused a terrible outcry in which the Jews proved themselves ready to die for their faith. The palace of Herod Antipas at Tiberias was burnt by the crowd, because it was decorated with the images of animals.

These extreme opinions were gradually abandoned, thanks in particular to the influence of Rabban Gamaliel. More tolerant than the other teachers, he was not afraid to go into public baths, although they were decorated with statues of Venus. "It is the statue", he said, "which was erected to embellish the dwelling, and not the baths built in honour of the statue".

Towns and villages were governed by severe magistrates. In every town there was a Sanhedrin of 23 members, if there were at least 120 men, or 3 members if the population was smaller than that. These Sanhedrin were appointed direct by the higher authority or High Sanhedrin, "The Council" of Jerusalem, comprising 71 members. It is difficult to establish exactly the limits of the power of these courts in criminal affairs. Of course, all ecclesiastical affairs and, so to speak, strictly Jewish cases—particularly religious questions—were within their competence. In every square there were what we might call municipal authorities, under the chairmanship of the mayor. These institutions, frequently mentioned in the Scriptures, were deeply rooted in Jewish society.

The administrative regulations on health were particularly stringent. At Caesarea, for example, there was a proper drainage system

that took waste to the sea. This was also the case in the buildings of the Temple at Jerusalem. In every town and villages rules of health and hygiene were enforced with the greatest severity. By law cemeteries, tanneries and some trades that could be harmful to public health had to be established outside the town, at a distance of at least 50 cubits. Similarly bakers' shops or dyers or cattle barns should not be set up under the roof of an ordinary house.

In building houses, no one could go beyond the line set for the facade. The streets were broader in general than those of the cities of the East until recently. The nature of the soil, and the position of several towns built on hills (at least in Judaea) offered certain advantages from the health point of view. It also meant that it was hardly necessary to pave the streets. Some towns were paved however—Jerusalem, for example—with white stones. In order to avoid any cause for conflict, inhabitants could not open their windows if they gave on to their neighbour's courtyard. It was also forbidden to place the main entrance of a shop in a courtyard used by two or three houses.

These few details give us a fair idea of life in a Jewish city. Take this street from a town in Judaea or Galilee. The houses differ in elegance or height. Over here is the house of a poor man which covers only 10 or 12 square yards. There is the sumptuous dwelling of a rich man; it is two or three storeys high, with rows of columns and architectural ornaments. Here is an upper class home, although it does not belong to a patrician. It is built of brick, unhewn stone or stone smoothed with a chisel; but marble has not been used and there are no sculptures. Its walls are not painted in any rich colours such as vermilion. They are quite simply

City wall fo Jerusalem (photo taken from the valley of the Cedron), with the Golden Gate and the orchards of Josaphat.

Below, one of the millenary olive trees in the garden of Gethsemane.

white or some very modest colour. A broad staircase, sometimes quite sumptuous, leads directly from outside to the flat roof whose very slight incline enables rain-water to drain away into a tank or cistern at the foot of the house. The terrace, paved with bricks or stones, is surrounded by a balustrade which, according to Jewish law, must be at least 2 cubits high (35 inches) and strong enough to take the weight of one person. Administrative regulations drawn up in the same spirit of solicitude prohibited the use of open wells or cesspools, unsatisfactory ladders, staircases in poor condition or even dangerous dogs roving round the houses. From the terrace of one dwelling to another there should be a regular means of communication, a way over the roof, so that a person could escape by going from one roof to another until he came to the last house, where he could go down the stairs leading to the bottom of the house without entering any one of them. For ordinary activities, the upper terrace was the coolest, airiest and quietest place.

Of course, it was sometimes used for the needs of domestic life. And by preference one went there to pray or meditate. You would watch, wait, observe the coming of a friend or an enemy, the approach of a storm. It was a vantage point for seeing the precise moment when the golden flame of dawn rose over the horizon. From here it was easy to continue a dangerous battle with an assailant in the street. A guest room was generally built on the very top floor so that the guest could enter or leave the house as he wished without being disturbed by the movements of the family. For the Feast of Tabernacles, shelters of foliage were built on the roofs in memory of the pilgrimage in the desert. There was an upper room, in which the family met to talk. Sometimes they preferred the courtyard below planted with trees that gave pleasant shade. When sitting in the covered gallery that circled the courtyard and on to which all the apartments opened, there came to the ears the sound of water trickling gently, a silvery sound of peace.

A staircase led to the upper terrace of the house. The main door gave access to the internal courtyard which was sometimes used by several families. A door-keeper would open the door to those who knocked once they had given their names.

After crossing the internal courtyard and the galleries, you came upon various rooms for the family, including a reception hall and bedrooms, with those furthest from the entrance for women. Then there were the inside rooms that were used mainly in winter. The furniture was much like what we use today. Tables, chairs, beds, candelabra, lamps varying in beauty and price according to the rank and wealth of the family. Among luxury articles there were plump cushions for the head or the arm; ornaments and sometimes even paintings. The doors in pinewood swung on hinges and were closed by wooden bolts that could be removed with a key. The dining-rooms were generally spacious and were sometimes used for parties.

The physical characteristics of an ancient Jewish city as we have just outlined them can be reconstructed from contemporary descriptions and archaelogical remains, but the lives of the people who inhabited the city are less easily resurrected from the dust of the past. In the case of the Jews, however, one circumstance facilitates the work of the historian. From biblical times to the present the characteristic genius of Judaism has taken the form of codes of law, the written record of God's commandments. The Jewish people, poor in creeds, are rich in statutes. The legal literature of the Jewish people is an especially valuable source for the historian because of its comprehensive character. The ever-widening distinction between the sacred and the secular has never found a place in Judaism, with the result that the provisions of Jewish law are equal in their scope and complexity to the demands of life—and of death.

The first Jewish law book was the Torah, a word that has many meanings; the word is sometimes used to refer comprehensively to the totality of God's commandments found in the first five books of the Hebrew Bible. To interpret and apply the frequently terse provisions of the Bible, however, there gradually developed a very extensive body of legal commentary, the Talmud, which over a very long period was reduced to writing. It is to the Talmud that one must turn to reconstruct the social life of Palestine in ancient times.

The word "Talmud" apparently stems from the Hebrew word "lomad", "learn" or "teach", and means "that which should be studied or taught". The Talmud is made up of two parts: the Mishna and the Gemara.

The Mishna is a collection of 63 treatises

One of the entrances of the Sanhedrin of Jerusalem. Below, a typical old village (forever famous): Bethlehem.

covering the oral traditions that supplement the written law of the Bible; it is a summary of Jewish ritual and jurisprudence. The name "Mishna" comes from the verb "shana" ; it refers to the fact that the Mishna is merely a repetition of traditional Law. The rules contained in the treatises of the Misha—traditions and ordinances—make no distinction between major and minor laws. Everything is divine. But there is no metaphysics; the code is absolutely practical. In simplest terms, what the Mishna contains is a set of civil, penal and ecclesiastical laws.

The Gemara is a compilation of: commentaries on some of the treatises of the Mishna; interpretations of legends, parables and doctrinal and ethical teachings; and speculations about the Scriptures.

Thus, it is evident that the Talmud covers not only social, moral, criminal, international, human and divine law, but also offers a picture of education, the arts, the sciences, history and religion for a period of about 1,000 years, and particularly of the time which immediately preceded and followed the birth of Christianity. It takes us through the jostling streets of Jerusalem, showing us the artisan at work, women in their homes, children playing in the market place, the priest and Levite celebrating their sacred rites, the preacher sermonizing on the hill, surrounded by a dense crowd, and even a popular story-teller in the bazaar; everything is alive, everything moves and breathes in these pages.

Upon starting life, the ritual of circumcision set the child of Israel apart from the surrounding nations and consecrated him to God. Pri-

Contemporary digs in Jerusalem and Meggido.

Left: antique house, perhaps the Simon the Currier house, mentioned in the Scriptures.

Opposite: lock of pre-Christian times and remains of a porch at Avdat, in the Negev.

The ritual pool at Massada.

vate prayers, morning and evening, sanctifying every day of life and the life of the family gave the home a marked character. Before every meal, the Israelites performed the ablutions and prayers prescribed by ritual. After the meal they said grace.

The return of the Sabbath sanctified the working week. The arrival of that sacred day was hailed with song like the coming of a young betrothed. Numerous prescribed rites were performed during the precious hours of this precious day of holy rest and joy for every family.

The observance of the Sabbath, however, was no simple matter. The Bible had simply proscribed work on the seventh day. But what activities did this proscription encompass? The elaboration of the lapidary biblical prohibition into a comprehensive system of rules and regulations affords as good an example as one can find of how the Talmudic scholars worked. Thirty-nine types of work were forbidden on that day, in order: 1. to sow; 2. to till the ground; 3. to harvest; 4. to bind sheaves; 5. thresh corn; 6. winnow; 7. clean fruit; 8. mill; 9. sieve; 10. knead; 11. cook; 12. shear wool; 13. wash it; 14. beat it; 15. dye it; 16. spin it; 17. weave it; 18. make a double cord; 19. weave two threads; 20. separate them; 21. make a knot; 22. undo it; 23. sew two stitches; 24. tear (the material) to sew two stitches; 25. take a kid; 26. kill it; 27. separate the head; 28. salt it; 29. prepare the skin; 30. scrape off the hair; 31. divide it into pieces; 32. write two letters; 33-34. build; 35. demolish; 36. put out a fire; 37. light it; 38. hammer an object together; 39. carry something from one place to another (Shabbat. VII:2).

Each of these points, in fact, raised some particular difficulty. Each required new explanations to be furnished by the rabbis. To what extent, for example, does the rule forbidding writing (32) apply? The sages reply: he is guilty who traces two letters with the right or left hand. It is of no importance whether he used for that purpose only one ink or two different inks; whether the letters are in one or several languages, whether he wrote them in a moment of forgetfulness or fully conscious of what he was doing; whether he used, instead of ink, colours, chalk or any other substance that leaves a lasting mark; but supposing the man wrote on two walls forming an angle, or on two pages of an accounts book. He is guilty "if one can read these two letters at the same time". This is not the case however "if he wrote it on liquid or dark coloured objects, on fruit juice or dust in the road, or sand, or on any object where the writing will leave no permanent trace". Then he is free from any transgression.

Take another commandment, that relating to putting out fires. This precept has been added to the law which only forbids the lighting of fires on the sacred day (Exod. XXXV:3) if a lamp is put out for fear of the Gentiles, thieves, or evil spirits, or to enable a sick person to sleep, there is no transgression. But if it is done to spare the lamp, the oil or the wick, the person so doing is guilty. (Shab. XI:5). A vessel may be placed under the lamp to catch the sparks from it, but water must not be placed there. This would be a guilty action, that of extinguishing a flame (Shab. XLI: 6).

Among the 39 forbidden labours was that of carrying any object from one place to another. The Sabbath is violated when a quantity of foodstuffs is carried equivalent to the weight of a dried fig, to the value of a mouthful of milk, to the quantity of honey necessary to cover a wound, or a weight of water equal to that needed to dampen the eye (Shab. VIII:1). It was also forbidden to carry a piece of paper large enough to write a bill of payment, a piece of parchment big enough to bear the smallest prayer in the Tefillin, enough ink for two letters. Rabbi Meir would allow a cripple to go out carrying his wooden leg but not everyone agreed (Shab. VI: 8).

It was also important to guard against any act that might lead to a violation of the Sabbath. When darkness fell on the town, the tailor was careful not to go out of the house with his needle, for he might forget and still carry it once the Sabbath had begun (remember that the Jewish day began at sunset). The scribe also had to take care not to go out with his pen (Shab. I:3). Care had to be taken to incline the lamp to give a greater quantity of oil to the wick. This could be serious because it would mean violating the commandment forbidding the lighting of fires. Climbing a tree or clapping hands were also violations of the law.

Something more serious. While the Mishna had made it permissible to help a man in danger of death on the Sabbath day, for example, by putting remedies into the mouth of any person suffering extreme pain in the throat because that might mean death for him (Ioma VIII: 6), this was not the case during the Roman occupation. Any healing on the holy day was a religious scandal for the strict observer of the prescriptions of the Torah (Matt. XII:9-13; Luke VI:6-10; XIII: 10-17; John V:1-15). The strict school of Shammai forbade tending a sick person or consoling a soul in anguish. Moreover the Mishna itself forbade on that day setting a broken leg or sprinkling cool water on a sprained and inflamed limb (Shab. XII:6).

As this skeleton summary of the Talmudic elaboration of the biblical prohibition of work on the Sabbath indicates, the rabbis were masters of the art of making the biblical text yield the final measure of its legal meaning. There are those, Jews among them, who have said, not without justification, that the process was carried to excess. In defense of the rabbis, however, it may be said that if they were ingenious in spinning out prohibitions, they could be equally ingenious in finding ways to circumvent their own rules. As the prohibition against carrying on the Sabbath, for example, would have had the effect of suppressing almost all freedom of movement on the Sabbath day, a way was found to get round the law. A narrow street or a space surrounded by buildings on three sides was closed off using a beam. This area then became a special kind of enclosure in which it was permissible to carry things without falling foul of the prohibitions laid down by the scholars (Erubin I:1s—VII: 6s).

One rule often brought to mind and as often violated, said that no one should go more than 2,000 cubits from his dwelling; that was called the Sabbath day's journey

Decorative motif of a capital in Capernaum.

(Acts I: 12), this being the distance from the tabernacle to the Israelite camp (Exod. XVI: 29). But a way was found to get round this precept. Anyone who wanted to go further on the Sabbath day had only to put enough food for two meals somewhere within the limit of the 2,000 cubits, for example at the furthest point. By this act, his domicile was situated at that point, and he could go from his real residence 2,000 cubits over the limit established by the law (Erubin IV: 7). Even this was not essential in every case. If an Israelite was already on his way when the Sabbath began, and he raised his eyes and saw a tree or wall at the distance of the Sabbath day's journey, he merely had to declare that that was his Sabbath residence and he could go not only to the place he had seen but 2,000 cubits further on. The statutory formula had, however, to be pronounced exactly. "My Sabbath domicile will be at that tree trunk" and not "will be under there". The expression would have been too general and too vague.

When the head of the family came from the synagogue to his home at the dawn of the Sabbath day, he found it decorated as for a feast. The Sabbath lamp lit up the house. The table was laden with everything the home had to offer. To begin with, he blessed each child, pronouncing over him the blessing of Israel. Then as night fell, the light of the Sabbath as it faded made a solemn separation between the holy hours and the week of labour. It was in the name of the Lord that the work of each day was taken up again. Strangers, the poor, widows and orphans were not forgotten. They were generously provided for. They also took part in these pious ceremonies which were not regarded as a burden, but as a privilege, and help was given them with great delicacy of feeling. All the people of Israel felt they were brothers. All could claim to be citizens of Jerusalem. Those who have studied Jewish life, its laws and customs at close hand, are well aware of this.

However all this has still given us only a very vague idea of religious life rather than family life. Firstly the very name given to a woman in Hebrew at her creation made her the appointed companion of her husband, as his equal ("Isha", woman, from "Ish", man). Study the relationships between men and women, parents and children, young and old, and you will see the immense difference between Judaism and the pagan religions. The idea by which God made himself known to his people calling him their Father was to give special strength to the bonds between earthly parents and their offspring. It was a sacred union.

No crime was more severely punished than a violation of the fifth precept of the Decalogue. The Talmud with its usual punctiliousness, enters into minute detail. It laid down the rule that a son is obliged to nourish his father, give him drink, feed him, protect him, lead him into the house, take him outside, wash his face, his hands and his feet.

Parents in turn took great care of their children. The latter showed their gratitude by putting up with their weaknesses, bearing with patience the caprice of the old man and his illnesses. Public opinion was trenchant on this point. Negligence in the fulfilling

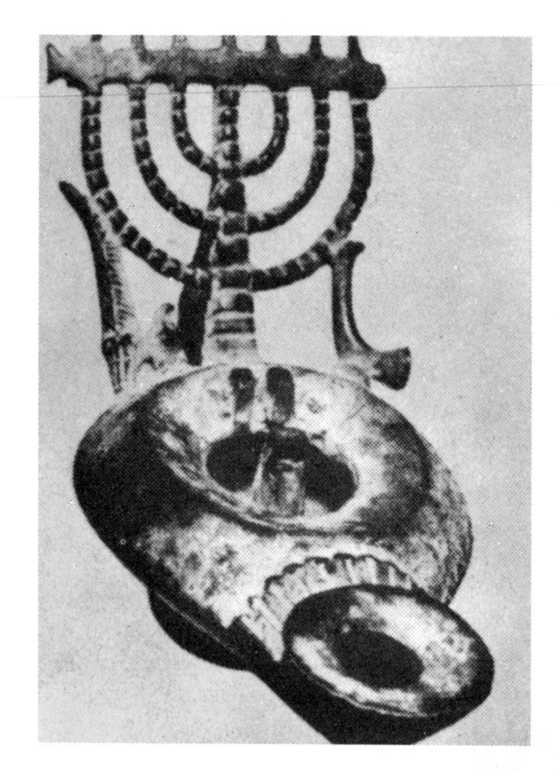

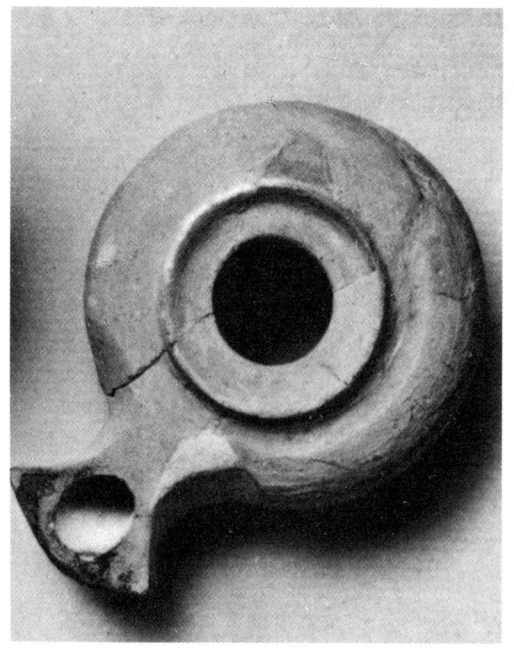

Religious lamps from pre-Christian times.

The central buildings of the Temple of Jerusalem and the reconstruction of an underground canal and one staircase giving access to it.

Below, well near the tomb of Rachel on the road between Jerusalem and Bethlehem.

of these duties, a lack of consideration and affection for those who had brought him into the world would have filled any Israelite with horror for the ignoble son. As for crimes towards parents, which the law of God punished most severely—they seem happily to have been almost unknown among the sons of Jacob.

The precepts of the priest clearly traced the duties of fathers and the limit of their power. A son who could earn his living was regarded as beyond their authority and although a daughter was under her father's authority until marriage she could not, once she had attained a marriageable age, be given to a husband without her consent, freely expressed. A father was allowed to chastise his child, but only when he was young and never to the point of destroying the feeling of personal dignity in him. It was forbidden to strike a child already grown up. Jewish law properly speaking limited the absolute duty of the father to feeding, clothing and boarding his child till the sixth year. After that age, he could be exhorted to fulfil this duty of paternal affection, but could not legally be forced to do so.

A few details on respect for the aged end this rapid sketch of Jewish life in the home. Although the exegetic exactitude may be doubted, the following teaching of the scholars is very fine: just as they said the broken tables of the Law were preserved in the Ark, thus great age should be revered and cherished, even when the mind of the old person or his or her memory had deteriorated with time. When the priests commanded respect for an old person who had no knowledge of the Law or who was a Gentile, they pushed condescension to the limit. However, opinions differed on this point. The Pentateuch said that men should honour old age and fear God, but this was applied only to men of science who alone could be regarded as ripe with age. One priest compared young men instructed in this august knowledge to those who ate green grapes and drank new wine. But Rabbi Jehudah taught that it was not the vessel one should look at but its contents. There were new vessels full of old wine and old wine-skins which did not even contain new wine.

4 - A deeply religious upbringing

Wedding scene.

We can see how powerful was the link between Jewish parents and their children by considering the large number of words in Hebrew which describe the various periods of youth. Besides the general terms "ben" and "bat", son and daughter, there are no less than nine expressions describing the stages of their development.

The newborn infant is a Yalud. Yonek is the suckling. Olel is the child being weaned. When he is Gamul, this process is complete and the occasion is marked with a solemn feast. At the period when the child is attached to his mother and tries to copy her he is known as a Taph. The Elim (in the feminine, Almah). Next be becomes a Naar, that is, shrugging off the yoke and assuming full freedom of action. Bachur is finally the grown-up adolescent and young warrior.

Should we not conclude from this richness of vocabulary that those who observed so closely the life of the child to the point of being able to paint in words the exact moment of development must also have surrounded him with loving tenderness?

There is a passage in the Mishna that describes very carefully the various periods of life. It is worth noting. Rabbi Jehudah, son of Temah, said "at 5 years, Bible reading; at 10, study of the Mishna; at 15, the young adolescent will begin studying the Talmud; at 10, study of the Mishna; at 15, the young adolescent will begin studying the Talmud; at 18, he will marry. At twenty years of age he will begin his commercial or industrial activity. At thirty, he will be in his prime: at 40, he will have maturity of reason; at 50, wise counsel. Sixty is the beginning

Hebrew mosaic inscriptions on the floor of the ancient synagogue of Ein Guedi. They express pious hopes for all the inhabitants of the city.

of decline; at 70, the hair begins to turn white; 80, old age; 90, the body stoops; 100, man dies and is taken from this world."

This passage is very clear. At 5 years of age the child should begin reading the Bible. But the opinions of the rabbis differed on this point. Genearlly speaking it was not considered wise to begin education so young unless the child had exceptionally good health and strength. Those who had only average strength or constitution did not begin work before the age of six. It seemed good sense and healthy experience that gave the following warning in the Talmud: if you set your child to study regularly before his sixth year, you will always have to follow him without managing to catch up.

A word in passing about circumcision. This was practiced by the Egyptians and the Ethiopians long before the Jews. Abraham established it among the worshippers of Jehovah, making a religious precept of a health measure, just as Catholicism did later for fasting in Lent. Circumcision was and is the Jewish equivalent of baptism.

It would be difficult to say exactly when the young Israelite began learning. Before the child could speak, before he could understand what he was being taught in the simplest language, before he took part in the rites of solemn celebrations during the week, in the sanctuary of the family, or in the august ceremonies of every year, his attention had been drawn by the Mesusah. This hung at the entranceway to every house. It was a sort of phylactery. It consisted of a square of parchment. The 22 lines covering it contained two passages namely Deut. 6: 4-9, and 11: 13-21. Enclosed in a shiny metal box, it was attached to the door-post. The child in his mother's arms naturally stretched out his hands towards it. He was all the more drawn towards it since he saw his father and other people touch the box with respect as they came in or went out of the house, then kiss their fingers with devotion, speaking the traditional blessing. From ancient times, in fact, the presence of the Mesusah was closely linked to divine benediction. The words of the psalm were applied to this venerated custom: "the Lord shall preserve thy going out and thy coming in from this time forth, and for evermore."

A very remarkable and indeed extremely ancient work, a venerable monument of Hebrew antiquity, a commentary on the book of Exodus (the basis of which is older than the Mishna itself since it dates from the beginning of the second century A.D. if not earlier), namely the Mechilta, makes a remark worth noting. It proves the efficacy of the Mesusah, showing that, since the days when the Angel of Death passed over the dwellings of the children of Israel, whose doors were marked with the seal of the covenant with Jehovah, the highest importance must be given to this sign which contained at least ten times the name of the Lord and which had been found in every home in Israel since time immemorial.

From the first awakening of consciousness in the soul of the child, the daily prayers of the members of his family, but especially the rituals of the Sabbath and the festivals, left an indelible impression on his mind.

In the early fall there was the very solemn

Day of Atonement, which was spent in prayer and fasting. The Feast of Tabernacles, the festival of thanksgiving, was celebrated at the time of the final ingathering of the harvest; for the holiday, temporary huts were built on the roofs of private dwellings and decorated with fruits. In the dark days of winter came Chanukah, the Feast of Dedication, when oil lamps were lit in every home in honor of the rededication of the Temple by the Maccabees. There was the gaiety of Purim, the Feast of Esther, which was filled with noisy joy. Then came the solemn Feast of the Passover. Now all the leavening must be thrown away. Every bit of food by its difference from ordinary food spelled out the fact that these days were different from all others.

Now the child is ready to receive some instruction. The days set aside for Jehovah. make a profound impression on him. None of those who went to worship in the house of the Lord in the holy city of Jerusalem could forget what he had seen, the words he had heard. In that splendid building, in the superimposed courtyards, the child looked with a mixture of wonder and religious awe at the crowd of priests in their white robes. He saw them celebrate the act of worship as the smoke rose from the sacrifices towards the sky. The offering of libation was sprinkled around and the singing of the psalms rose from the Levites like thunder echoing round the valley of Cedron, mingling in it gentle harmony, the clear piercing voices of the children of the priests with the deeper tones of the mens' voices accompanied in sweet accord by musical instruments.

The Jewish child knew most of the words of these songs. They were the first songs he had heard when as a "Taph" he clutched at his mother's gown. Now in the courtyards of the Temple of Zion decorated with marble, covered with glinting gold under the blue vault of the sky, they fell upon his ears like the echo of another world, the thrice repeated trumpet sequences of the priest seeming to awake some long lost memory. And were they not in fact the calls of a higher world that he was hearing? As his father had taught him, was not everything here below made after the image of heavenly things that God on Sinai had shown to Moses? The words he heard ring out had been pronounced by Jehovah through his servant David and the other cantors of Israel.

In the darkness of the holiest sanctuary where the High Priest entered only once a year, dressed in a simple white robe and not in the gold-encrusted vestments he usually wore, lay the holy ark. It contained the tables of the law on which the man of God had traced the immovable ordinances of Holiness.

How could the child forget the impression he felt on seeing the first sacrifice of the Passover celebrated, remembering that memorable night when Israel was born to national life? Then they became a people redeemed by the Lord. At a certain moment during the meal, the youngest child would rise from the table and ask what the rites being celebrated meant. His father would reply, in a language accessible to the child's intelligence, recounting the national history of Israel from the call of Abraham until the deliverance from slavery out of Egypt. He

Remains of Haran, small town in Iraq, where, in the ruins of a temple and a palace dating from about 1500 B.C., writings of the IInd century before the Christian era have been found, relating many customs in accordance with talmudic tradition.

described how the divine law had been communicated by the Lord to His people on Mount Sinai.

The historian Philo, recalling these details, could say without exaggeration that the Jews, from their earliest childhood, before even being taught the religious laws or traditional customs of Israel, learnt from their parents and their masters to acknowledge God the Father and to see in him the creator of the world. Instructed by the knowledge of the law from their earliest years, they bear engraved on their souls the perfect image of the commandments of Jehovah. Josephus is no less precise in his testimony. From the earliest moment of their awareness, they learn the law in such a way that the divine precepts are indelibly printed on their mind.

In many passages in the Scriptures we find exhortations to parents regarding the education of their children. The object of this teaching was to acquire true wisdom, fear of Jehovah, obedience to his laws, while negligence of these precepts led to misery

Right: a Jew on a bas-relief at Memphis.

strikingly portrayed by the holy writer. There is a teaching summed up in an aphorism: teach the child the path he must take and when he is old he will not deviate from it.

The Book of Proverbs offers an extremely interesting doctrine. It accords women the dignity which is theirs and acknowledges their rightful influence within the sanctuary of the family. The father was mainly responsible for the upbringing of the child; the law of Moses and the ordinances of the Rabbis jointly imposed this duty on him. But it is clear in the story of the patriarch that the woman had her usual influence on the soul of her son, particularly in his tender years. It is a natural consequence of the relationship between them.

Although rich people alone had a complete copy of the Bible, written on parchment or on a scroll of papyrus, the most humble family guarded like a precious treasure a portion of the divine word, the five books of the Law, a Psalter, or a scroll containing the writings of one of the prophets.

The Talmud says that there came a time when small parchments were made available for children. They contained important extracts of the Holy Word. The Shema, the Hallel, the history of the origins, the flood, and the first eight chapters of the Book of Leviticus.

At aged 13, according to the Rabbinic laws, the child was received as Bar Mitzvah or "Son of the commandment". From then on he was an adult member of the community and was subject to the obligations of the divine precepts and enjoyed the privileges they provided for their religious observers.

Safad, old inscriptions on the wall of a synagogue.

5 - School

No religion of any of the advanced civilizations of antiquity proved that it was capable of guiding men along the straight and narrow path—except for that of the Jews.

A strange thing. Outside Israel, it was almost impossible without desecrating the words to talk about family life or even the family as we understand it. Perhaps the following is significant. Tacitus, the great Roman historian, points out a particular detail, namely that among the Jews it was a crime to put a small child to death.

This is not the place to discuss the exposure of infants or diverse crimes through which ancient Greece and Rome at the height of their civilization rid themselves of those young lives that were regarded as a useless part of the nation. Only a very small number of those who have learnt to admire classical antiquity have a complete knowledge of all the details of the social life of the time. Many cultivated men have only a very sketchy idea of the position of women, relationships between the sexes, slavery, the upbringing of children, their relationships with their parents, or public morality.

When we leave the pagan world to enter the home of the Israelite, we are struck by the intense exclusiveness that we meet. It is like leaving the nerve racking heat and dazzling light of the tropics to enter into a room full of pleasant shade, the welcome coolness of which makes us momentarily forget that the shade is perhaps too deep. This exclusivism applied to everything that came from outside: to religion, family life, social and even studies honoured among the pagan people. At the time of Christ, for example, a pious Jew was ignorant of and did not seek to know any ways except the way of God. He declared all else anathema. In paganism, theology or rather mythology had no influence on thought. Far from ennobling moral life it tended on the contrary to lower it. For the faithful Jew, knowledge of God was everything. The supreme aim of upbringing and education was to acquire it by study and spread it by teaching. This was the life of his soul. Everything else including bodily existence was subordinated to this higher life, the only true life. Everything should serve man as a means to attain the end for which God had created him.

The main object of the religion of the Israelites was first and foremost knowledge of Jehovah. By a series of deductions, this led to a highly developed theological science, with minutely detailed prescriptions of a cult laid down by the law, and to practical acts of charity towards others. These observances could go beyond strict obligation (Chovoth) to reach a degree of special merit or "justice" (Zedakah). Theology was therefore at the basis of religious life. It was the highest of all sciences and higher merit was given to those who cultivated such knowledge.

A young Rabbi asked his uncle if he might not study the wisdom of the Greeks since he already knew the Torah in its entirety. His uncle replied in the words of Joshua: "Thou shalt meditate therein day and night"; "Go now", added the old Rabbi, "and see what hour there is that does not belong to either day or night. If you find it you may use that time to study the wisdom of the Greeks."

It is quite clear that according to the law

of Moses, the father was responsible for the child's early education. The mother was doubtless responsible for directing his first steps. If the father was incapable of giving such elementary instruction, then someone outside the family was called in. Education in the home generally began at about the age of three. Before this, the infant's memory was already exercised. This faculty has always been particularly developed among the Jewish people. The child was taught verses of the Bible, blessings and sayings of the sages; mnemonics were invented to help the young children remember what they had learned. Tremendous importance was attached in fact to learning the exact words of the tradition. The Talmud describes the ideal student by comparing him to a well-cemented tank, which does not leak a single drop of the water it receives. According to the Mishna, whosoever by negligence forgets a single point in his study of the Mishna, the Bible holds him guilty declaring that he has failed "in the proper use" of his life.

To teach the alphabet, letters were drawn on a board until the child had become familiar with them. The master would then, point out with his finger or with a stylus, the model letter to be read, in order to keep the child's attention. It was expressly forbidden to use a manuscript that was not completely free of mistakes. It was rightly thought that once a child had absorbed false ideas in the beginning, they were very difficult to eradicate. At age 5 or 6, the pupil began to read the Bible in Hebrew, beginning not with Genesis but with Leviticus. The most likely reason for this rule is that Leviticus

Ruins at Capernaum. On the following pages: the stele of Mesa (musée du Louvre, Paris), bearing the oldest known inscription in Hebrew, and the mosaic floor of the synagogue of Beth-Alpha with signs of the Zodiac (c. 500).

Ruins of the Nabataean era at Avdat.

contained the ordinances that an Israelite had to know from his earliest years. As for the history of Israel, he had been inculcated with it for a long time by word of mouth and it had been continually repeated to him during the holy festivals and in the synagogue on the Sabbath day.

Writing was much less widespread a skill than reading. Israelites were certainly familiar with writing from the earliest period of their history. Perhaps they acquired it during their stay in Egypt. Words were engraved on precious stones decorating the breastplate of the High Priest. The various genealogies of the tribes were reproduced. This skill was not exclusive to the priests, but was fairly general among the people. It is known, for example, that copies of the Law were made. The Book of Joshua mentions a prophecy in "the book of Jasher"; and we are also told that Joshua "wrote there upon the stones a copy of the law of Moses".

In a later period, the word "scribe" shows that there had become a need for this special class of writers.

The priests were opposed to giving girls the same education as boys. They did not approve their studying the law, either because they believed that a woman's duty or mission should preferably be exercised in another field, or because the subjects studied were not ones that girls could deal with suitably, or perhaps because the studies would have caused familiarity between the two sexes, which seemed morally undesirable.

The child received his education in his home, where he learned the commandments and the ordinances and, as expressly stated

Left, one of the famous manuscripts known as the Dead Sea Scrolls. Below: ancient Hebrew parchment. Below right: detail of the first of the manuscripts shown opposite.

Right: this sealed paper is a contract and the inscription says that the deed relates to a house.

in the Talmud, was taught to repeat the traditional prayers aloud. He knew them perfectly because of the very use he made of them. When aged 6 he went to school. This was not the Academy, or "Bet ha-Midrash", where he could take courses only if he had the proper aptitude. He also could not be accepted in the class of a famous Rabbi and could not attend discussions of the Sanhedrin. Such privileges were for the most advanced pupils. Here it is a matter of primary or elementary school such one-room schools (heders) were attached to each synagogue.

Every locality that had 25 pupils of suitable age or, according to Maimonides, 120 families, was obligated to pay the salary for a primary school teacher. He was for his part forbidden to have more than 25 pupils. If there were 40 pupils, the teacher had to have an assistant; if there were 50, the leaders of the synagogue arranged for him to have two assistants.

These details help us to understand the doubtless exaggerated figure of the number of schools in Jerusalem. At the time the city was destroyed there were, we are told, no less than 480 schools in the metropolis. One author even attributes the fall of the Jewish State to the fact that children's education was neglected—which just shows the importance popular opinion attached to it.

"Go up and down before their Houses of Study and Houses of Worship. If you do not hear the voices of their children chanting, you can overcome them. But if you hear the chanting of their children, you can never subdue them."

6 - The Jewish Woman; Marriage Customs

For a proper understanding of the position of women among the Israelites, it is enough to make a careful study of the Scriptures. From the picture of social life given us by the holy writers, we see that she is not confined to the gynaeceum as was the custom in the East from earliest times. She mixes freely with the inhabitants of the home and meets strangers. She is not an inferior. She often has a very important role in moments of agitation, particularly religious crises. We do not find her having disorderly private or public habits. In Israel, the woman is very often pure, the home peaceful, the family sanctified by religion. Religion was not simply a few public ceremonies; it entered into everyday life.

A few details give a better demonstration of this than any long dissertation. Take the explanation by a rabbi of woman's creation from one of Adam's ribs. "It was as if Adam had exchanged an earthenware pot for a precious jewel." The Jew liked to repeat with gentle irony, "God cursed woman, however everyone runs towards her; he cursed the earth, however all men live by its products." Sarah, Rebecca, Leah and Rachel, "the four mothers" according to the expression of the priests, were very highly regarded; and no one who has read the Bible can be unaware of the authority they had at the time of the patriarchs.

Then there are the women whose hearts were touched by the divine light and wisdom. They helped to build the Tabernacle. Deborah freed the people from slavery and judged Israel. The piety of Manoah's wife is as outstanding and more intelligent than that of her husband. And what of Samuel's mother? During the period of the Kings, the praises of the young girls of Israel aroused the jealousy of Saul; Abigail managed to save her house from the storm threatening it through the folly of her husband. And was it not a wise woman who ended the rebellion of Sheba? The fact that queen mothers are mentioned frequently because of their habitual intervention in government shows us how high a position they held. The name of Huldah the prophetess, the touching story of the Shulamite come to mind. And what of Ruth? This whole book is the story of one woman's loyalty and devotion. The pure and faithful love of a woman is the theme of the beautiful descriptions in the Song of Songs. A woman's courage is the basis for the Book of Esther, while the last chapter of the Book of Proverbs lists the values and the virtues of a strong woman.

Take a look at the prophets. They call the people of God "the daughter", "the maiden", "daughter or Zion", "daughter of Jerusalem", "daughter of Judah". The relationship of this people with the Lord is time and again compared to the relationship between husband and wife. The terms used in the Scriptures to describe woman are deeply significant. The word for, woman "Isha" which is simply the feminine form of "Ish"(man), confirming the equality between them. A man who commands, is known as Gever; the woman within her usual field of activity is known as "Geverah" or "Geveret", the mistress.

Although the practical process of divorce was relatively easy, the priests tried to hedge

A very old Jewish tradition: a father blesses his daughter the day before Yom Kippur "among the qualities a woman must have were above all gentleness, modesty and shame."

it round with conditions which in more than one case could prevent its taking place. The tendency of the laws of Moses was to recognize the rights of women, even considering those who were slaves. In legal battles, the law weighed in their favour.

The words of Malachi show what the feelings of the Jews were on this subject at the time of the prophets. He points to the altar of God covered with the tears and weeping "of the wife of thy youth; the wife of thy covenant"—"And this have ye done again, covering the altar of the LORD with tears, with weeping, and with crying out, insomuch that he regardeth not the offering any more, or receiveth it with goodwill at your hand. Yet ye say, Wherefore? because the LORD hath been witness between thee and the wife of thy youth, against whom thou hast dealt treacherously: yet is she thy companion, and the wife of thy covenant... therefore take heed to your spirit, and let none deal treacherously against the wife of his youth."

This passage is paraphrased as follows by the priests: "If death has taken the wife of thy youth, it is as if the sacred city and the very temple in the days of a pilgrimage were besmirched, torn down and covered with vile dust. For the man who brusquely rejects his wife, the affectionate wife of his youth, the very altar of Jehovah weeps bitter tears."

Relationships between boys and girls were fairly free. The young man usually chose his own wife. The Scriptures give various examples. The woman in every case had to give her free consent before the betrothal or marriage. Without such consent the union was not valid. Minors, in the case of girls 5 under 12 years and 1 day, could be betrothed or given as wives by their fathers. In this case they had the right to ask for divorce later.

The story of the sons of Eli tells us what was the outcome of marriages inspired by desire for riches. They sacrificed everything to the passion for gain. And their posterity was such that it would crawl in the mud for a coin or a bit of bread. As for marriages contracted by the desire for honour, take the story of King Joram, who became the son-in-law of Ahab. When Athalia his widow saw that her son Ahaziah was dead, "she arose and destroyed all the seed royal". How different are those marriages celebrated in the name of heaven. Children born from such marriages are the guarantee of the eternal life of Israel.

It was fairly usual for two forms of the same verb, which had almost the same meaning, although spiritually—if not very reverentially—to be used to express two very opposing ideas on marriage. The newly married husband was asked: "Maza or Motze?" that is "he finds"or "he is found" alluding to these two passages: to find a wife is to find happiness; and I shall find something more bitter than death, the wife whose heart is a net and whose hands are chains. It is a quite different example from that of the Talmud but there is an immediate analogy with the following statement: he who loves his wife as his own body, honours her more than his own body. He raises his children in the path of justice and guides them on it to their maturity. Such a man, the Scrip-

Statuettes from Canaan.

tures tell us, will truly know happiness in his tent. Among the required qualities of a woman were gentleness, modesty and shame. A liking for quarrels, chattering in the street, a lack of modesty in public were sufficient reasons for divorce. Of course no Jewish woman would ever have thought of teaching in the synagogue, where she had a separate place from the men. The priests declared that he who allowed himself to be governed by his wife would call but no one would answer him.

For a similar reason, the Synagogue claimed that the man should seek out the woman and not *vice versa.* But the reasoning is strange. Man was made from the earth, woman from man's rib. In seeking a wife, he is only trying to find what he has lost. The origin of man was soft clay, that of woman dry bone, and this according to the Jewish scholars is the key to a difficult question. It explains why man is more willing to be reconciled to his enemy, woman, than she with him. The teachers also said that God did not form Eve from Adam's head, for fear that she should be proud, nor from his eye, for fear that she would be envious. Had she been taken from his ear, she might have been curious. Taken from his mouth, she would have been a gossip; from his heart she would have been jealous. Formed from his hand, she would have desired the goods of others; from is foot, she would have carried trouble and disunity everywhere. She was taken from is rib because this part of the body is always covered by clothing. Therefore cannot you see that modesty is the supreme quality she must have?

It would be impossible here to go into all the details of Jewish legislation on marriage, dealing for example with property or capital that might come to the woman after betrothal or the celebration of the wedding. The law assigned them to the husband. Despite many accommodating arrangements for the wife, the laws hesitantly recognised the right of the stronger.

The Mishna tells us about Shitre Erusin or documents of betrothal. They were drawn up by the administrative authorities and the costs were met by the young man. These contracts stipulated the mutual obligations of the betrothed, the dowry and other points on which the parties had come to an agreement. The Shitre Erusin differed from the regular Chetubah (literally, writing) or marriage contract. In the absence of this act, the priest regarded the union as merely legalised concubinage. The Chetubah provided for a deposit of 200 denarii for the young girl, and 100 denarii for a widow. This sum was raised, by a council composed of the members of the clergy of Jerusalem, to 400 denarii for the daughter of a priest. These figures represent only the legal minimum deposit which could be raised indefinitely, according to the desire of the contracting parties. Opinions however differed when it was a matter of determining whether larger sums could be legally claimed by one of the parties when the steps taken had gone beyond betrothal.

According to Jewish custom, the young man married his wife "according to the law of Moses and Israel". He promised to please her, honour her, nourish her and take care of

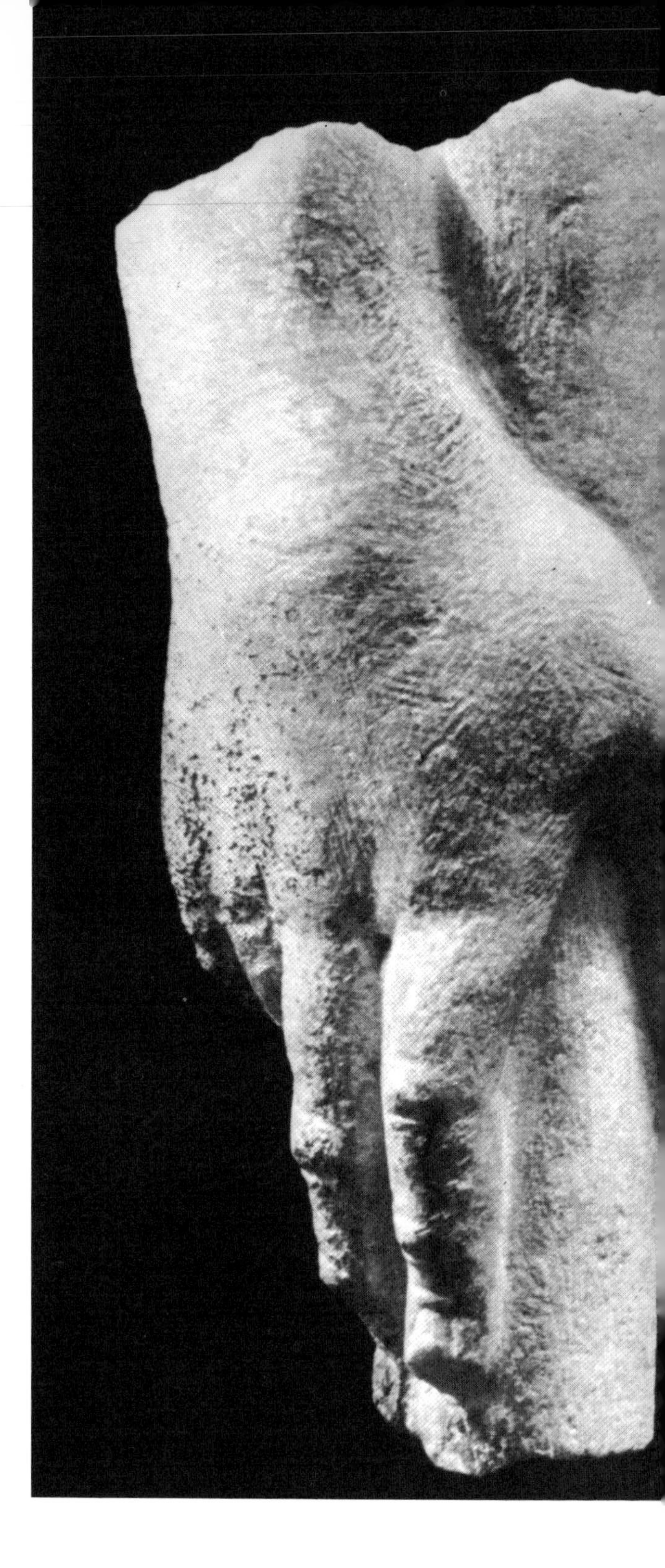

Marble found in the catacombs of Beth-Shearim. Right, Jewish coins showing the Menorah (candlestick).

her as was the custom among the sons of Israel. The young woman gave her consent, and the contract was signed by two witnesses. This was in all probability the form used in ancient times. In Jerusalem and in Galilee, it was often said that a man's choice was determined by the beauty of the woman, while in the rest of Judaea men attached particular importance to the dowry. A widow was assured of the right to remain in her husband's house.

The girl's father was obliged to give his daughter a dowry (nedan, nedanjah) according to his position. A second daughter had the right to demand as much as her elder sister, or else one-tenth of his immovable assests. At the father's death, the sons, according to Jewish law the only heirs, were obliged to provide for their sisters, even when this duty reduced them to penury. They had at the same time to allot them one-tenth of the inheritance. The dowry, money, property or jewels was mentioned in the marriage contract and in fact belonged to the woman. It was felt that the husband should add one half above its value in money. If the dowry was in jewels, he gave his wife four-fifths of their value. Should they separate later (not divorce), he was obliged to give her the necessary means to live, and to receive her at his table and in his home on the evening of the Sabbath. The wife could claim one-tenth of her dowry for her incidental expenses.

When a father gave his daughter to a husband without any mention being made of the amount of the nedanjah, he had to allot her at least 50 zouzim. If it was expressly stated that she would receive no dowry, the law sagely ordered the young man, before the celebration of the marriage, to present her with whatever she needed to be properly dressed for the occasion. As for the orphan, she received a dowry of at least 50 zouzim from the ecclesiastical authorities.

A husband could not force his wife to leave the Holy Land or the city of Jerusalem, nor to leave a town to go and live in the country or *vice versa*. He was forbidden to force her to change a good house for a dilapidated dwelling. All these matters were usually discussed at the time of the betrothal (Tenaim, a binding agreement), which was celebrated with some solemnity. To break the engagement or wilfully to defraud the

Two peasant women and a young donkey on the road to Jericho: as in Biblical times.
An ancient fountain at Ain-Karim (where John the Baptist was born).

other party at that time was sufficient reason for the union to be dissolved once formed. With the exception of special cases, only divorce proper could break the link between the two espoused.

According to the teaching of the priests, some formalities were required to make the betrothal valid in the eyes of the law. The young woman had to receive, directly or by messenger, a coin, however small, or a letter. In each case, it was supremely important for it to be stated in the presence of witnesses that the man had the intention of marrying the young woman concerned. After a period of time laid down by legislation, the marriage was celebrated ("Kiddushin", sanctification). The young wife was led to the home of the husband with great pomp and ceremony and according to certain customs dating from the earliest times. The marriage of a young girl was usually celebrated on a Wednesday afternoon; this meant that the necessary preparations could be made in the first few days of the week. The husband who had any complaint against the behaviour of the young Israelite could, on the other hand, take them before the Sanhedrin which sat every Thursday. As for the marriage of a widow, it took place on Thursday evening.

The wedding ceremony was naturally followed by rejoicing. This was why it was not held either on the Sabbath, or the day before it or the day after it. The holy day of rest reserved for the Lord had to be kept free from the slightest echo of disturbance. It was prohibited by law to be married during one of the three major feasts of the year. The priests said that earthly pleasures should not be mingled with holy joys. It was a religious duty to make the newly wedded couple happy. It appears that in their zeal, gaiety sometimes went beyond the limits approved by the strictest scholars.

The wedding ceremony began by a blessing preceded by a short formula by which the young girl was given to her husband. The two young people were then led to the nuptial couch. The girl at that moment loosed her hair.

Usually women had to keep their heads covered and hide their hair. When a woman was accused and found guilty of adultery, her hair was cut or her head shaved. The following formula was used: "Because you have scorned the customs of the daughters of Israel, who walk with their heads covered, what you have chosen has happened to you." This may be a throw-back to the ancient faith of the Israelites who believed that evil spirits came to dominate women who went bare-headed.

The use of a veil worn by the wife, or spread over the young couple, goes back to primitive times. It was forbidden by the priests for some time after the destruction of Jerusalem, together with the custom of wearing crowns which was older still. Palm and myrtle branches were brought before the young couple and grain or money was spread around them. Musicians led the procession in which it was considered a religious duty to join.

A divorcee could not marry her seducer, nor could a man marry the woman to whom he had brought the letter of divorce, or for whom he had given evidence in her case.

Marriage was forbidden to those who were mentally deranged, minors and men in a state of drunkenness. A widower had to wait until three feasts had passed before remarrying, a widow three months. If she had a child, or if she was suckling, she had to wait 2 years before contracting a new marriage. No woman could marry for a third time. No marriage was allowed within the 40 days following the death of a relative.

A priest had to find the legal ascendants of his wife (to the fourth degree if she was the daughter of a priest, to the fifth degree in any other case) unless the father of his fiancée was a priest in active duty or a member of the Sanhedrin. The High Priest could only marry a virgin who had reached puberty less than 6 months before.

Divorce was very easy to obtain. Any kind of misbehaviour, the habit of loosing her hair, spinning wool in the street, over-familiarity with men, unkindness to her husband's relatives in his presence, quarrelsomeness, that is to say talking to her husband so loudly that the neighbours could hear, a bad reputation, the discovery of a fraud committed before marriage, all these were sufficient reasons for divorce. The wife could ask for divorce if her husband had leprosy, or a polypus, or practised a dirty or disagreeable trade such as tanning or boiler-making. Divorce was obligatory when one of the parties became a heretic or had ceased to profess Judaism.

Left and right, capitals at Capernaum (200 B.C.).

Black lava millstones from the time of Christ.

7 - The Law of Work and Rules of Trade

"Let every man" said one priest, "teach his child an honest easy trade, calling on him from whom comes all wealth and riches. There is no trade in fact that does not have both rich and poor, and it is not the trade itself that causes poverty and wealth. Both are dispensed according to the person's own merits." Rabbi Simeon, son of Eleazar: "Have you ever in all your life seen an animal or a bird engaging in any traffic? They nonetheless receive what food they need, without the worries which beset us. Well! these being created only for my use have the constant care of a vigilant providence. Cannot I therefore expect to find the means of subsistence without being eaten out by worry, I who have been created to serve my creator and my God? But if I do evil, I lose the right to be helped by the hand of Jehovah." Abba Gurjan of Zadjan declared on behalf of Abba Gurja: "Let no man raise his son to be a leader of asses or camels, a barber or a sailor, a shepherd or pedlar. These are the trades of thieves."

The following comes from the Mishna: "To what can we compare the man whose knowledge exceeds his manual labour? He is like a tree with many branches and few roots. A wind gets up, tears up the tree dashes it to the ground. But he whose acts are greater than his knowledge, to what shall we compare him? To a tree with few branches, but many roots, even if all the winds dashed against him, they could not tear him from his place in the earth."

There are other maxims showing the dignity of the worker. When Adam, according to the Talmud, heard the sentence of his creator "thorns and thistles shall the earth bring forth to thee", he burst into tears. "What!" he cried. "Oh Lord of the world, shall I eat at the same rack as the ass?" But when the following words rang in his ears: "In the sweat of thy face shalt thou eat bread" his heart took courage. Such, according to the priests, was the dignity of work. Man was not forced to do it, and he does not do it without being aware, but by becoming the slave of the earth, he draws from the very ground the precious fruits of the golden harvest. Work feeds him who does it. This is the basis for the law requiring the thief of an ox to give it back plus four times its value, while for a ram only three times the value was demanded. Why this difference? Because the ox helped man in carrying out the task to which God had called him.

The Mishna states in principle that a father should not teach his son a trade which will force him to have *constant* relations with the opposite sex. Such occupations are those of jeweller, perfumer, weaver. The latter had a lot of difficulty with the demands of their customers. It was said that the weaver must be humble or his days would be shortened by excommunication. In other words, he had to bow and scrape to everyone to earn his living. A Scottish proverb says that even the weaver is master in his own home. That was how the Jews felt about it. "Although a man may be only a wool carder, his wife will present her request at the door of his dwelling and will sit respectfully by him," she is so proud of her husband. "I am," said the priest of Jabne, "simply a man like my neighbour.

He works in the fields, in the town. We both get up in the morning to go to work. Where in all this can you see a cause for placing one of us above the other? Do not think that one does more than another, because we have learnt that there is as much merit in doing small things as great things, provided our heart is whole." "A man," we learn elsewhere, "who dug reservoirs and built basins for the ablutions ordered by the law, one day went up to the High Priest Jochanan and said "I am as respectable a man as you". In fact in his own field, he was making as much a contribution to the good of the community as the most learned scholar in Israel.

Any poor worker could appeal to the members of his trade association and he was helped until he had found work. The tinmen or boiler-makers association had a leather apron as the sign of their trade. When their members went abroad, they took a collapsible bed. This society had its Rabban or leader in Jerusalem; it had a synagogue and a cemetery. The workers of Jerusalem were of outstanding skill. One valley, that of Tyropeon, was occupied by dairymen. Hence its name "Valley of the Cheese-makers". Isaiah 7: 3 mentions the fuller's field. It lay "at the end of the conduit of the upper pool". The Talmud contains a list of sayings known by the title "Proverbs of the Fullers".

The princes of the family of the Herods, lovers of beautiful buildings and external splendour, had many artisans constantly working on the building of magnificant monuments. When the Temple was rebuilt,

The pool of Siloam.

there were no less than 18,000 workers employed on different jobs and some of them very skilled artists. Herod the Great had employed a large number of the most experienced so that they could teach their art to a thousand priests, who were in turn responsible for building the Holy of holies. Nothing could be left to lay hands in the building of this part of the Temple. In the sacred enclosure, there was no sound of a hammer or an axe, or a chisel or any iron instrument. "Iron," says the Mishna, "shortens the life of man. The aim of the altar (made of stones drawn from virgin land) is to prolong it. How could it be proper to use something which diminishes on something which gives greater duration?"

Time has marched on since antiquity, but men have not changed. Bosses were told then: "Do not eat better quality bread and give black bread to workers or servants. Do not sleep on feathers and give them small beds strewn with straw particularly if they are your co-religionists; whoever acquires a Hebrew slave has given himself a master".

The idea of mutual insurance seems to have been known among muleteers and sailors. They would return to its owner an animal or vessel lost without negligence on the part of the owner. We can even find the first hints of a trade union in the permission given by the Talmud to workers to work only one or two days a week so that all the artisans in the city could find work.

Again in this connexion we can see how the priests explained the Scriptures: the words "he does no harm to his neighbour" accord-

An ivory of Samaria.

ing to them referred to the worker who did not concern himself with the affairs of his companion at work.

There were certainly good reasons for this change in the ideas of leading Jews, who went from scorning manual labour to expressing considerable enthusiasm for it, sometimes to the point of affectation.

As long as the people were independent, at least nominally, as long as they possessed the country of their fathers, manual labour as a form of occupation for a whole lifetime was viewed with some disdain. They regarded it as indicative of a lower social trade status or of a person only concerned with the things of this world. It was quite another matter when the empire of Judaea passed into the hands of foreigners. Honourable work was the only way of achieving the independence worthy of man. To do this work insofar as it was necessary to obtain the result, to try and not need anyone, to be able without shame to raise one's head in the presence of a friend or an enemy; to sacrifice to God one's natural inclinations, strength and time, to have the faculty of devoting oneself freely to the study of the divine law, that was a very fine resolution. And it brought its own reward.

The priest Gamaliel made the following recommendations: "Be careful in your relationships with powerful men. They only think of getting to know someone in their own interest. In the hour of need, you would seek their support in vain." Rabbi Maththja said: "Greet every man peacefully, and prefer to be the tail of the lion rather than the head of the fox." In other words, honourable independence achieved through individual effort.

The scholars expressed themselves very differently regarding trade. The general fervour with which the people of Israel later threw itself into business and thus earned so much reprobation, stemmed from a considerable change in the social environment, and from an unavoidable need. Dispersed by the hundreds of thousands among other nations, a poor conquered homeless minority without strength, the Jews, avoided with scorn, trodden underfoot, scapegoats for every popular displeasure, could only find a way open to them in trade. In many places, Jews were forbidden to own land and were excluded from the crafts guilds. They were forced to become tradesmen and to become active in commerce because it was the only type of work that they were permitted to do.

Nothing in ancient times particularly marked Israel for a trading people. The many restrictions against relationships between Jews and Gentiles laid down by the law of Moses on its every page are sufficient proof of this. The implementation of the law of Leviticus prohibiting the loaning of money for interest would have made all commercial transactions impossible, although this law was not as absolute in regard to people living outside Palestine. The law of the Sabbatical year and that of Jubilee, in their turn brought commerce to a halt. The country was not very conducive to the coming and going of the business necessarily involved. It is true it had long coastlines, but the whole coast, including the ports of Joppa, Jabneh, Ascalon, Gaza and Ptolemais, belonged to

Site of Caesarea.

the Philistines and the Phoenicians except for a period. At the time when Herod the Great built the beautiful port of Caesarea, the roadstead was used almost exclusively by foreigners. This is the conclusion that the history of Israel leads to. Once during the reign of Solomon, we see an attempt made by the people to enter into large-scale trade. We are told that the merchants of the king imported horses and spun wool. This seems to show the existence of a kind of royal trading company or a monopoly for the sovereign. Solomon has even been described as the first large-scale "protectionist". We know that he built a fleet at Etzion-Geber on the Red Sea, a port conquered by David. These ships traded with the Phoenicians at Ophir. These political acts of the son of the prophet-king were in direct opposition to the designs of God as contained in the Scriptures. They did not have any important results. As to the attemps made by King Jehosaphat to start up trade relations again with foreign peoples, they led to disaster His vessels were shipwrecked at Etzion-Geber and shortly afterwards this port fell again to the Edomites.

Josephus says exactly what his compatriots thought when he writes: "As far as we are concerned, we do not inhabit a maritime country. We take no pleasure in trade, we do not like dealing with foreign peoples as merchants. We live in built-up cities far from the sea; the country where we live is fertile and we spend all our effort on the cultivation of the soil." This was the attitude of the priests. In the 73 treatises that make up the Talmud, there is hardly one word in favour of trade. There are, however, 100 passages showing the dangers to which anyone who wishes to enrich himself by trade is exposed. "Wisdom,"

says Rabbi Jochanan explaining Deuteronomy 30: 12, "is not in heaven–that is to say, is not to be found in those whose soul is filled with pride. Do not seek it 'beyond the sea', that is, among men given to business and in the midst of merchants." Then there are the precautions that the Jewish law took against professional moneylenders or usurers. So we can read in the Rosh Hashanah 1: 8, "Here are the men unworthy to give testimony, the dice player (gambler); the usurer, breeder of pigeons (for betting or bait); those who trade in the products of the seventh year and slaves." Even more pungent is the following: "God said in speaking of the slanderer: this world is not big enough for both of us."–"The usurer takes away a piece of the man, because he takes what he has not given him." It is interesting to note a few other sayings. Rabbi Meir says: "Go with care (do little) in trade, but study the Torah zealously." "Keep clear of business": this is one of the 48 qualities that anyone who wishes to acquire the knowledge of the holy law must have. Take finally the words of Hillel: "He can never become wise who plunges himself into the worries of many enterprises, and in a place where there is no man; try to be yourself and to be worthy of this name."

Weights and measures inspectors are a fairly recent introduction in the West. The Rabbis were well in advance of us on this point. They had several servants responsible for going from one market-place to another and establishing the current price for merchandise. The value of the product was determined by each commune. Few merchants subjected themselves to this interference by the civic authorities in the law of supply and demand. But the Talmud was extremely severe with those who bought all the cereals, and removed them from commercial transactions, particularly in time of shortage. There were harsh penalties for artificially forcing up the price of goods. This particularly applied to the products of the soil. Anyone who took more than 16 per cent profit was regarded as an absolute scoundrel. It was in general forbidden to exploit abusively the essentials of life. Deceit earned the guilty person more severe punishment than the violation of any other precept of the moral law. These latter faults could be made good by repentance. But the man who deceived his neighbour wronged not only one person or several persons, but all the citizens. How could one make reparation for such a sin? Everyone was encouraged to remember that God punishes even those faults which escape the eye of the human judge.

We were talking about the changes in the feelings of the Rabbi caused by the changes in the situation of the nation itself. They are very clearly expressed in the Talmud. "The Israelite must divide his money into three portions. With the first, he will buy a dwelling in Palestine. He will use the second to acquire certain goods (with which he may do trade) and he will keep the third, in coin, in a chest. "But", it goes on "remember this consolation. Among the joys of the world to come there is one more precious than all the others. There will be no more trading. "

Left: ruins at Meron. Below: coins (enlarged) from various times in the pre-Christian era. "Strange to tell, nothing particularly destined Israel to be a trading people... ».

As for this life, if he goes into business, the pious man can use the interest made to help the sages in their work. He will imitate the example of a certain Sebna, one of the three wealthiest men in Jerusalem, made famous for the care he took of the great Hillel. This brings us to an obvious conclusion. The rules applied to the Jews of Palestine and of Babylon; they did not concern the Israelites of the "diaspora". For them, trade was a necessity, the main way of meeting the cost of their existence. This was particularly applicable to the wealthiest community, the Jews of Alexandria.

A strange, very dramatic story is that of the Israelites in this great city. Long before the Babylonion captivity, Jews had poured into Egypt. This memorable catastrophe in the history of the nation, and later, the murder of Gedaliah swelled the number of emigrants. But the exodus really began under Alexander. This monarch granted to the children of

"For the Jews of the diaspora, trade was a necessity... This was particularly true for the richest community, that of Alexandria." Below: reconstitution of a rich Egyptian dwelling.

Israel, as inhabitants of the city that bore his name, the same rights as the Greeks resident there; he thus raised them to the rank of a privileged class. Their number gradually increased; their star was in the ascendant. They commanded the Egyptian armies, influenced the translation of the Scriptures into Greek. There is no time here to talk about the Temple of Onias at Leontopolis, which rivaled in beauty that of Jerusalem, nor the magnificence of the great synagogue of Alexandria. At the time of Philo, there were no less than 1 million Jews living in Egypt. In the city of Alexandria, they occupied two of its five districts, which were known by the first five letters of the alphabet; furthermore they obeyed leaders they had themselves chosen in almost total independence. The delta district, that ran along the coast was almost exclusively theirs; officials responsible for surveying navigation on the sea and the river bordering their district, they held sway over the huge export trade, particularly that of grain—and everyone knows that Egypt was the granary of the world. They provided cereals for Italy and the Old World. During the troubles in Rome, the Jewish bankers of Alexandria were able to receive reliable political news from their correspondents, when no one else had yet heard it. This enabled them to plump for Caesar or for Octavius and to reap the political and financial results of this skilful move.

Exactly what was the trade of the Jews, and what rules governed it? The pedlar who went from one country to another limited himself to exchanging the products of the first against those of the second. Fish from Spain, apples from Crete, cheese from Bythinia, lentils, beans, pumpkins from Egypt and Greece, wine from Italy, beer from Media, crockery from Sidon, baskets from Egypt, clothing from India, sandals from Laodicaea, shirts from Sicily, veils from Arabia, such was the merchandize brought into Palestine. Wheat, oil, balm honey and figs were exported. The value of exports and imports was almost the same, but the balance tipped slightly in favour of the Holy Land.

The protective trading laws provided for the smallest detail. Some of the treatises of the Mishna are full of painstaking information on this point: "the dust of the balance" is a strictly Jewish concept and saying. The law laid down that a wholesale merchant should clean his measures once a month, and a retail merchant twice a week. All the weights had to be washed once every 8 days and the balances wiped after each use. For the buyer's complete security, the seller had to add one ounce to the weight of goods at each sale of ten pounds (lbs) in the case of a liquid, and half an ounce in the case of a solid. The affair was not regarded as concluded until the contracting parties had taken possession of their belongings. But when one of the contracting parties had received the money agreed, the other would be guilty of dishonour and sin if he refused to execute the contract. If the price were excessive, or the profit higher than it should be, the buyer had the right to take back the articles sold and claim the excess he had paid, provided that he returned to the merchant within a

Left, woman's head, painted on a fragment of pottery from Heigh Antiquity, found at Beth Shean. Below, Jew taken into captivity, on a bas-relief at Thebes.

Opposite and below: Israelite figures on a very old bas-relief showing the deportation of the Jews. "Be cautious in your dealings with powerful men... in the hour of need, their help is sought in vain."

short period of time (which should not be more than the number of minutes necessary to show his purchase to another businessman or relation!) The law protected the seller with the same care. A moneychanger could make a fixed charge for changing small coins and return the money in a given time, if it was below the weight at which it had been accepted. It was forbidden to force a merchant to say what was the lowest price at which he would sell his goods, if the person asking the question did not have the serious intention of buying. Nor could you remind him of the inflated price he had asked for an article for the purpose of making him lower whatever he was asking at this moment. It was a serious offence to mix articles of different quality, even when those added to the original mass were of greater value. To protect the buyer, farmers were forbidden to sell wine diluted with water in Palestine, except in cities where this was a custom known to all. One priest even condemned merchants who offered children little presents with the aim of attracting their parents' as customers. All of the scholars regarded procedures used to make the article for sale appear to be of a higher quality than it was, as wilful deception. No wheat could be sold until the general tariff for the market had been established.

The rabbis were extremely careful to avoid even the appearance of usury. A woman, on borrowing a loaf of bread from a neighbour, had to establish its value at the time, for fear that a sudden change in the price of flour should force her to pay more than the value of what she had borrowed. If a house or a field was leased, a slightly higher price could be asked if the money was not paid in advance to the owner, but not in the case of a sale. As for interest (which the Romans calculated monthly) security, or behaviour towards insolvent debtors, nowhere is the moderation of Jewish law equalled. It was, with some restrictions, permissible to accept a pawn and to sell it in case of non-payment. But for this purpose only clothing, bedding, carts and utensils for the preparation of food could be accepted. It was prohibited to accept a pawn from a widow or to sell what belonged to her.

A careful study of the customs of the nations around Palestine and the cruel demands of Roman law would show the appreciable difference between Israel and the Gentiles. The more one meditates on the code of the scholars of the Synagogue, the more one is forced to admire their farsightedness and wonder at their wisdom and delicacy of approach.

A turbulent style—like so many aspects of Israel—this capital of the synagogue of Capernaum shows a sculpture of the famous candlestick.

8. Clans and Sects

It was impossible to go through Galilee or Judaea without coming face to face with a singular personality, quite different from all those around him. It was the Pharisee flattered or feared, avoided or sought out by admirers, looked on with respect or unmercilessly railed against, the Pharisee was a power in the synagogue and in politics everywhere, because he had attached himself to the most influential, the most zealous, the most closely linked society. This association spared neither time nor effort in pursuit of the aim it had glimpsed; it feared no danger and stopped at nothing. The name Pharisee is familiar to anyone who has studied the history of the Jews. But there is no subject on which about so many fallactes have been written, and also no subject which throws more light on the history of Judaism.

There was probably no town or village inhabited by Jews that did not have some Pharisees. Generally speaking, however, they preferred not to go far from Jesuralem. The Temple, and what was perhaps dearer to the hearts of all members of this powerful association, its 480 synagogues, as well as its large and small Sanhedrin and schools, held them there. It is not difficult for us to recognize the man we have just met. So let us follow him. It will not be long before the hour of his prayers obliges him to stop. Do you see him stop suddenly on his way? He is repeating a portion of the prescribed prayers, now he is going on again saying another fragment. What does he care if everybody notices his acts of worship in the public square or at the street corner! He will stop, as the law of tradition demands, position his feet according to the ordinance, adopt the required attitude, drape his robes as they should be; then he will bow deep so that every vertebra of the spinal column will be separated from its neighbour. The worker will leave his tools, the street porter will lay down his burden, the horseman will take his foot from the stirrup, the hour has struck and nothing must interrupt or disturb its peace. Should a king pass by and greet him, he would not answer the greeting, and he is forbidden even to trouble himself about the snake that has wound round his heel.

It was not only the time laid down by the law for prayer which demanded that he should perform the required devotions. On entering or leaving a village, he had to pronounce one or two blessings; he had to do the same when crossing a fortress, at a time of danger, and when he was faced with a new, strange or unexpected sight. The longer the prayer, the greater its value. In the eyes of the rabbis it had two advantages, since a long prayer is sure to be heard, and abundant prayers prolong life. Special religious merit was attached to each of these prayers, which ended with the blessing of the name of God. His expression, a mixture of deep satisfaction, mocking modesty, ostentation and gentleness, betrayed him before even the minute detail of his action, the care he took to avoid contact with people or things he regarded as impure, and his extravagant show of piety demonstrated his singular quality. Clearly we are talking about only the class or the party of Pharisees and its tendencies and not all the members that constituted it. It must not be forgotten, as we shall see further on, that there were many degrees, from the most humble Pharisee who was only initiated to the first observances the novice to the most advanced of Chasid. The latter for example was in the habit of making a sin offering every day for the faults he might have committed.

How far did the scruples of the most advanced among them go? There was a priest who did not want to allow his son to remain in the operating room with a surgeon for fear that he would be soiled by contact with the member that had been amputated and which was therefore a dead body. Another Chasid went so far in his observance of the Sabbath that he refused to rebuild his house because he had thought of that undertaking on the holy day. Some of them said you could not give a letter to a Gentile for fear he might deliver it on the Sabbath! These are real examples, without exaggeration of Pharisaic practices and thinking.

The clothing of the Pharisees was of course different from that of the other Israelites. However simple the dress of antiquity, it must be remembered that, even more than in our time, wealth, rank and luxury were obvious among the inhabitants of Palestine. The polite Greek, the courtier of Herod, the rich Sadducee, and many of the society women who protected the Pharisees were easily distinguishable in the crowd. The Jewish writings give us such detailed descriptions of their toilet that we could easily join the fashionable society of Tiberias, Caesarea, Jerusalem or of the Jews of the "diaspora" in Alexandria or the wealthy cities of Babylonia.

No less than 18 articles were needed for an elegant toilet. The material, colour and cut of his costume distinguished the wearer. The poor man used a blanket as a coat and at night it kept out the cold. The elegant gentleman wore a very fine, white, richly embroidered robe, and sometimes a purple robe with a curiously chased silver belt. The decoration of this costume consisted of a border that the Pharisees liked to have as wide as possible. The undergarment fell to the heels. The head was covered with a kind of pointed hat or a sort of turban wound and intertwined with varying degrees of artistry. The ends often fell gracefully down the back. It was customary to wear gloves to keep the hands from contact with the air or anything dirty.

The women used various kinds of veils. The Arab veil allowed the wearer to see everything around her without difficulty. This veil, which was a part of the clothing, was a kind of mantilla thrown gracefully around the body and covering the head. The Egyptian veil covered the breast, and, was often of precious metal garnished with jewels. Sandals consisted of soles strapped to the feet. Noble ladies also wore richly embroidered slippers decorated with stones and so made that with a little pressure of the foot perfume was given off. Perfumes and scented oils were very common. The latter were prepared from oil mixed with the essences of Palestine, or some which came from far-off countries, making them very expensive. The most valuable of them were kept in alabaster jars.

The perfumer's trade was nonetheless

regarded with scorn by the Jews and the pagan people. High society made liberal use of oils and baths to increase the strength and vigour of the body. The hair, beard, forehead, face, even the garlands to be worn during feast days were oiled. And that was not all. Some women used cosmetics. They painted their cheeks, darkened their eyebrows with a mixture of antimony, zinc and oil. Their hair, considered one of the attributes of beauty, received great care. Young women wore it long. For men it would have been regarded as effeminate. The beard was carefully combed and perfumed. Slaves could not wear a beard. As for young peasant women, they tied up their hair very simply. But the society Jewesses curled, plaited and decorated their hair with gold and pearls. Their favourite colour was a kind of chestnut. It was often produced with dye, or by sprinkling gold powder in the hair. We hear of false hair and false teeth. There were pins and

Detail of the signs of the Zodiac shown on page 73.

elegant combs for the hair. And we learn without surprise that some dandies had artistic hair-dos. The occupation of hairdresser was no more highly regarded, however, than that of perfumer.

The men usually wore a seal attached to a ring or hung around their necks. Some had bracelets worn above the right wrist; these were usually made of ivory, gold or precious stones. Fashion-followers among the ladies wore bracelets and also rings on their fingers, in their hair, and in their noses; sumptuous hairstyles, necklaces, chains, not to mention flat earrings decorated with pendants and sometimes a little bell. The nose ring, which by the law of tradition had to be taken out on the Sabbath day, hung over the upper lip in such a way however that the wearer could still greet privileged friends. Two kinds of necklaces were worn, one fitting close to the neck, the other of precious stones or pearls fell over the breast and sometimes to the waist. A fashionable woman wore two or three such chains on which she hung scent dispensers, ornaments or even pagan talismen. Golden pendants were attached to the hair, which was sometimes piled up like a tower. As for ankle bracelets, they were arranged so that together they sounded like a lot of little bells. Often two ankle bracelets were joined together, forcing the person wearing them to take very small steps. There were also gold and diamond pins. All these descriptions are borne out by documents of the time. This gives us an idea of elegant society.

What has been said above helps to clarify the contrast that must have existed between a Pharisee and the crowd around him. Austere and hard, or insinuating and sugary in his approach, he carefully avoided any contact with those not of his society or those who held an inferior position.

His costume alone betrayed him. Divine law ordered the wearing of edging on the bottom of robes as a holy memorial. It had to be blue, symbolic colour of the covenant. But the Mishna authorized the wearing of white. Every pious Israelite attached it to his undergarment. The mystics of Judaism later discovered analogies between the edges decorated with bright bands and the way in which the Schechinah wore the works of creation. Imbued with this law, the pious Jew covered his head with this mysterious piece of clothing during prayer.

Although the custom of wearing edging on clothes was authorized by the Scriptures, we cannot say the same for the phylactery. Some people have see the origin in Exodus 13:9, "And it shall be for a sign unto thee upon thine hand, and for a memorial between thine eyes, that the Lord's law may be in thy mouth." The special term used by the Rabbis to describe the phylacteries, Tefillin or prayer band, is of comparatively modern origin. In any case while every Israelite male wore them only to say prayers or on solemn occasions, the Pharisees wore them all day long.

Tefillin were worn on the left arm, facing the heart, and on the forehead. This ornament consisted of cubes, which contained writings on parchment (that on the forehead on four different parchments), the four passages from the Scriptures: Exodus 13: 1-10; 13: 11-16; Deut. 6: 4-9 and 11: 13-21. These little

Pre-Christian perfume flask.

cubes were attached by black leather straps that were crossed round the arm (7 times) and fixed to the forehead in a certain way prescribed by tradition and which had a mystic significance. There was no mistaking anyone who wore them. Their value and importance in the eyes of the priests cannot be exaggerated. They venerated the Tefillin as much as the holy Scripture. Like the latter, they had the power to save them from the flames on the Sabbath day. It was said that Moses on Sinai had received from God the law requiring Israel to wear them. The Tefillin were more holy than the golden plaque on the forehead of the High Priest, since on the latter the name of Jehovah could be read only once, while the passages written in the Tefillin contained this holy word more than 23 times. The commandment ordering people to wear them on the forehead and around the arm was considered by some to be equal in value to the divine precepts taken together. Some people even supposed that God himself wore phylacteries.

Let us get back to the Pharisees, who saw themselves as representing the divine law, not only that given to Israel on Mount Sinai, but the secret ordinances given to Moses orally and which, by explaining the Torah, formed the necessary complement to it. If they had raised a barrier around the Law, it was purely for the benefit of Israel. They wanted to cut it off from everything impure and from the Gentiles. The Pharisees were bound by the strictest vows. Their work, their way of life, their gait amidst those frivolous crowds, those Greek immigrants, then so numerous in Judaea, earned them

Jerusalem: two views of the Mount of Olives. "If I forget thee, O Jerusalem, may my right hand forget her cunning."—"If I do not remember thee, let my tongue cleave to the roof of my mouth."

Jerusalem: the grottos of the Valley of the Cedron (left) and view of the city, taken from the Garden of Olives... "There will I make the horn of David to bud."

the highest places on the feast days, the main seats in the synagogues, salutations in the street, and the sweet joy of being called by young and old "Rabbi!" ("my master!")

In fact the members of this party represented to a certain extent all the fervour and religious zeal in the holy country. Their name, which they probably did not use themselves, had for some become a nickname, for others the name of a party. Unfortunately in many cases, they betrayed their original purpose. They were not necessarily scribes, men of the law, or the masters who taught it. It was also impossible to regard them as a sect in the real sense of the word. In this society with members of various degrees, there were novices admitted as such, and all the associates were bound by special vows and duties. They entered into the association by heredity, as it were.

Everyone knows that their principles often predominated, and that they gave the teaching and practices of the synagogue their particular stamp. But one thing which shows how strong their influence was is that to achieve these results they needed only a handful of disciples. It seems incredible and it has not been said often enough that the number of associates at the time of Herod were no more than 6000, and yet this minority cast Judaism in its own mould of thinking.

Two vows were imposed on association members: to pay the tithe and remain free of any impurity. In practice this raised innumerable questions that the laws of Moses did not resolve.

Hence the need for traditions regarded as additional explanations of the Hebrew code.

Blind guides were often by the members of the party. The phrase "plague of Pharisees" was often heard and, lumping them together with the pietists, clever sinners and the Pharisee woman, they made a group of unbearable creatures that were called the burden of the trials of existence. "Should we waste time explaining the opinions of the Pharisees?" asks one Rabbi in extreme scorn. The Sadducees said that "little by little the Pharisees will subject the brilliant globe of the sun itself to their laws of purification". Side by side with such rigour, there are numerous sayings that reek of epicureanism, such as: "Make haste, eat and drink, for the world in which we live is like a betrothal feast." "If you have something good, derive from it all the pleasure it can give you, for there is no pleasure under the earth, and relentless death pursues its destruction in humanity." "Men are like flowers of the field, some open with the light of day, others fade and disappear."

The Pharisees became so powerful that even their adversaries, the Sadducees, were obliged to submit to their authority. The latter maintained that on the Day of Atonement the High Priest should light the incense before going into the holy place. As this was a custom contrary to the teaching of the Pharisees, they forced the High Priest to take a vow to observe their form of ritual before allowing him to celebrate the holy offices. According to the Sadducees, daily sacrifices should not be paid for from the public treasury but levied on a treasury that had

Two old Jews, indigenous to Palestine.

collected special contributions. The Saducees had to defer however and take part in the half-day feasting that the triumphant majority had written into the calendar in order to perpetuate the memory of a contrary decision. According to the Pharisees, people should count the days between the Passover and Pentecost, beginning on the second day of the feast. The Sadducees claimed that they should literally be counted from the Sabbath following that day. What did the Pharisees care? Despite their arguments, the Sadducees had to join in the solemn procession which on the afternoon of that day was going to cut the first sheath of corn.

The Sadducees wanted to stick to the letter of the law doing neither more nor less than it ordained, whatever the consequences. This was the rule they applied, to points of jurisprudence as well as to matters of religious doctrine. We cannot enter into detail, of course, but clearly such literalism necessarily made their legal decisions (or rather those they proposed) much stricter than the Pharisees'. They demanded nothing less than the careful application of the principle

A phylactery: the compulsory amulet of the Pharisees.

"an eye for an eye, a tooth for a tooth." This point of view covered anything from the law of purification to that governing heredity.

The origin of the word "Sadducee" raises many difficulties. All the etymological explanations are unsatisfactory. It is sometimes connected to the high priest Tsadok. Again it is attributed to a priest of this name whose principle was that one should never seek for reward when fulfilling the duties imposed by religion. This was an idea they had little understood and badly applied. Some experts regard the word "Tsadikim," the just, as the origin of the name of this religious group. Although incomplete, each etymological explanation offered contains some element of truth.

Beyond a shadow of doubt the society of the Sadducees was formed in reaction to Pharisaism. The latter added their commentaries, interpretations and traditions to divine law. The Sadducees based their lives on the letter of the law. They wanted nothing to do with any of the additions, they refused to be excessively just. For them it was enough to practice "Tsedakah," justice.

Be that as it may, the men who opted for the opinion of the Sadducees belonged in particular to rich aristocratic families including the opulent houses of the priests. The mass of the people and particularly women respected and supported the Pharisees.

Josephus and Philo mention a kind of ascetic order, the Essenes. Their influence on Jewish society was slight and they rapidly disappeared. They can be viewed as a sort of very extreme Pharisaic group, associated with worship and practices deriv-

Upper part of door of the synagogue of Bir-Am.

ing from the mysticism of the East and more particularly the Medo-Persian religion. In the Essene philosophy, one of the aims was a higher purity. A careful study of their doctrines, comparing them with the system of Zarathustra, shows how much they had borrowed from the East. As everybody knows, the philosophical and religious ideas of Persia had a considerable influence.

As a sect, the Essenes never numbered more than 4,000. They lived retiringly, did not mix with the society of men nor join in divine worship. Generally speaking, they did not marry: thus they soon disappeared from the face of the earth. The writings of the priests mention a certain number of people introduced as sectarian and who all more or less belonged to the Pharisees, practising mysticism and asceticism. There were the Vathikin, the strong. They held prayers at daybreak. The Tobleschachrith, the morning baptists, immersed themselves completely in water before morning prayer, in order to pronounce the name of God when in a state of perfect purity; the Kehila Kadusha, or holy assembly, devoted one third of the day to prayer, one third to study, one third to work. The Banaim, or builders, pursued the aim of higher purity, and at the same time engaged in mystic studies of God and the world. The Zenuim, or pious hidden men, kept their doctrines and their writings secret. The Nekijehadaath, in turn, men of pure mind, lived separate from their fellows. There were the Chashaim, or men of mystery, and the Assiim, the men who helped and healed souls and who claimed to possess the true pronunciation of the sacred name of Jehovah and naturally all the blessings which flowed from such knowledge.

In some cities of Judaea, you would meet with men dressed entirely in white. They wore sandals and clothing that were already showing signs of age, because they could not throw them away until they were no longer wearable at all. Their clothing was however scrupulously clean. These were the Essenes. The passer-by would stop and look at them with a mixture of respect and curiosity. It was rare to meet them in towns or villages. The sect lived quite separately from the rest of the nation in desert areas, particularly around the Dead Sea. They observed the Sabbath in their own synagogues and had gifts for the altar taken to the Temple, but did not attend themselves. They offered no sacrifices, either because they felt that the ordinances of the sanctuary were not sufficiently pure from the point of view of Leviticus, or because they considered their own table as an altar and their meals, taken together, as a sacrifice.

Religious orders, they were governed by strict vows taken under exacting oaths and subject to the severest discipline. They abstained from wine, meat, and also oil. Most abstained from marriage. They professed the joint ownership of goods and were bound by vows of poverty, chastity and obedience to their superiors. They were especially exhorted to be truthful in speech. They could not swear an oath, and they could not have slaves. There were four degrees of initiation. Contact between the member of a higher degree with a member of a lower degree sullied the more advanced of the two.

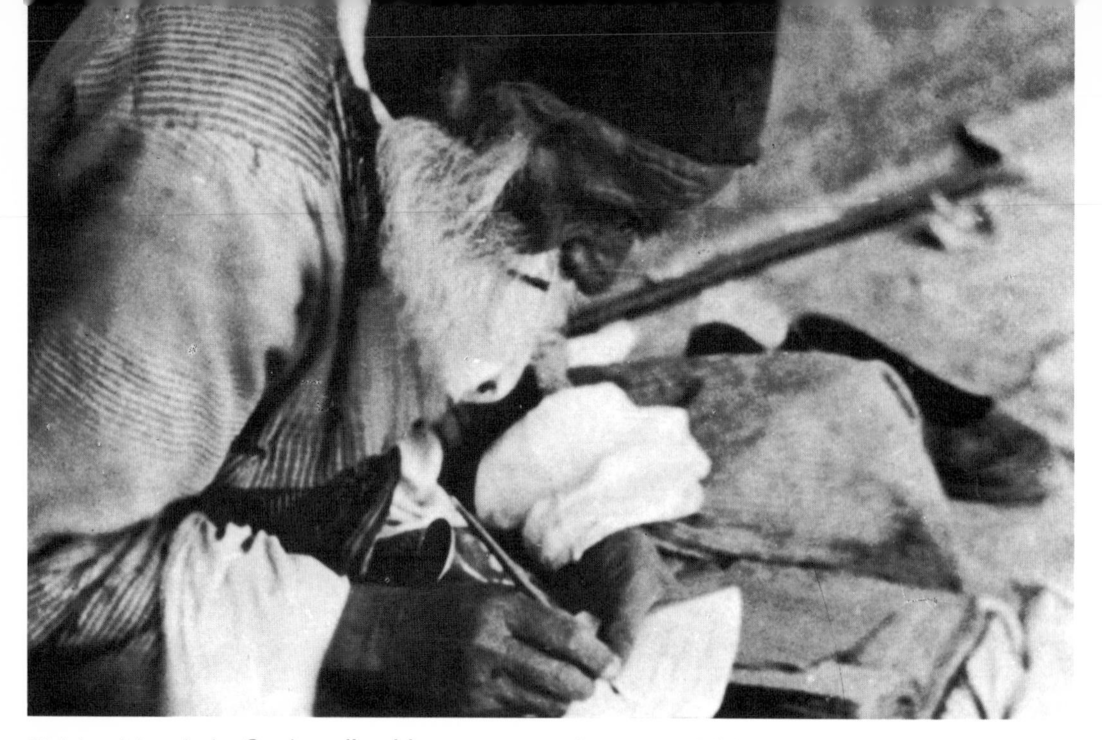

Old Jewish scholar Sepharadi writing commentaries on the Bible.

Although the noviciate lasted 2 years, the candidate was accepted into closer communion with the members of the society after the first year. The elders, who had the power, had the right to admit or exclude any member. To be excluded was equivalent to death by starvation, because the Essene was obliged by a strict vow never to enter another society.

For the Essenes, the day began at sunrise. They met for prayer. Before this religious duty, they could not speak about mundane things. Once prayer was over, they busied themselves with agricultural tasks, since they themselves were not allowed to have pastures and flocks; they did acts of charity, particularly healing the sick. At 11 o'clock they bathed, and changed their clothing. A priest opened the service and closed it with a prayer. Everyone had his place according to his age and rank. The most aged could converse among themselves, but fairly quietly so that they could not be heard from outside. The young people were servers. Everyone received bread, salt and another dish. The elders could use hyssop as a condiment, and had the right to take hot water. After the meal, they changed clothes, and continued work until the evening. There was another meal taken together, followed by hymns and mystical dances symbolizing the ecstacy and the joys of the spirit.

These mystic sects were the depositaries of certain doctrines on divine essence, the Messiah and his kingdom, which later emerged in the secret traditions of the synagogue. Some have attempted to trace the descent of Christ and the New Testament from Pharisaism or to find some relationship between his teaching and that of the Sadducees and Essenes. There were undoubtedly some similarities. But according to other Christian thinkers, there was no real basic analogy between the religion of Jesus and the communities around him.

Below, figure engraved in the wall of the catacombs at Beth Shean.

9. The Synagogue

Rabbi Jochanan said: "Whoever prays in his own home, surrounds it with an inviolable barrier; he fortifies it, as it were, with a wall of iron." But he pointed out that this principle held good only for someone living in a lonely place. Wherever there was a community, prayer should be offered up to God in the synagogue.

The origin of the synagogue is lost in the obscurity of tradition. The Rabbis trace it back to the patriarchs. In the Targum of Jonathan and in that of Jerusalem, we see Jacob attending worship in the synagogue, and Rebecca too goes to hear the holy directives when she feels the struggle between the two children she is carrying.

No town or village with 10 men which could or wanted to apply itself to things divine was without a synagogue. Why would 10 be the lowest number of men required for a congregation? The reply of the Rabbis is as follows. According to the statement in the Book of Numbers 14:27: "The evil congregation" consisted of spies, who had brought dreadful news on their return from the land of Canaan. There were 10 of them, if you leave out Joshua and Caleb.

The largest cities, such as the city of Jerusalem, had several synagogues according to Acts 6:9.

When a stranger entered a town, he easily found a house of prayer. There were perhaps no slender bell-towers whose pinnacle seemed to carry the thoughts of all those in their shade heavenwards. But synagogues were built on the highest places as a clear symbol showing that the study undertaken within them had a higher aim than the mis-

Left, a capital, in the ruins of Capernaum. Right, stele c.1200 B.C.: Is not this the very symbol of prayer?

Throne of a synagogue in Galilee.

erable objects of human preoccupation. They recalled the word of the prophet: the house of the Lord shall be set upon the high mountains and raised above the hills.

When such a site could not be found, then a corner position was sought, or an entrance to the main square in accordance with the passage: "wisdom cries at the entrance of noisy places, at doors in the city she makes her word heard". If there was no high ground on which to build a sanctuary, a beam was placed on the roof to raise it above the tallest houses. Any town whose house of prayer was lower than the other dwellings was regarded as in danger of ruin.

We can get some idea of the architecture of these buildings from the oldest synagogues that still exist and from recent digs in Palestine. Inside they were rectangular or circular. Around the nave was a single or double colonnade decorated with sculptures. A sacred symbol was chiselled outside on the lintels of the door: usually the seven branched candlestick or the urn that held the manna.

It was considered a serious fault to pray behind the synagogue without turning towards the building. There is a story told of Elijah who appeared in the form of an Arab merchant and punished a man guilty of this sin. He told him, "You stand before your master as if there were two powers or gods in the universe." Scarcely had he finished saying this than he drew his sword and slew him.

Another unique custom was that a person should walk the length of two doors down the nave before stopping to pray. This prescription derived from a passage in the Book of Proverbs. "Blessed is the man that heareth me, watching daily at my gates, waiting at the posts of my doors."

The Talmud counsels people to leave the assemblies slowly, but to go them at a brisk pace since it was written, "let us go on to know the Lord."

In general, the synagogues were built by contributions from the congregation, sometimes helped by the richer members of the group. It was not unknown for a devout believer to bear the cost alone. This was a particularly worthy act. In other circumstances, when there were few Jews, a large room in a private house was set apart for this purpose.

Synagogues were inaugurated and consecrated by solemn prayer. The ceremony was not regarded as complete before the ordinary requests had been offered by one of the faithful, even if he was only a stranger passing through the locality. The congregation had to observe rules of decency similar to those in use in the Temple of Jerusalem. The need to wear suitable clothes was stressed, as was composure and respect in the attitude of the body. There was a wealth of detail. Collections had to be consecrated to the poor or to buying back captives. If the building was near to ruin, it had to be demolished on condition that another would be raised in the same place as soon as possible. Even so, the holiness of the place was respected. It was forbidden for anyone to string up ropes or nets, or fruit in order to dry them. The money collected to build one of these houses of prayer could, in the case of absolute necessity, be used by the congregation for another pur-

This painting of the Roman catacombs is thought to be the oldest representation of the Holy of Holies. Below: the tomb of Moses.

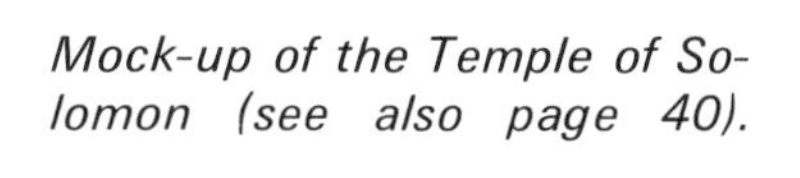

Mock-up of the Temple of Solomon (see also page 40).

pose. But if the stones and beams and so on had already been bought to begin building, these materials could not be put on sale again. They were regarded as consecrated to God. The synagogue was inalienable in a town or city, but in a village it could be done away with according to the opinion of the local Sanhedrin provided that the site was not being used for public baths, a wash-house or reservoir. The product of the sale had to be used for something more sacred than stones and mortar, namely for the expense of maintaining the ark in which the copies of the Law were kept.

Separation of the sexes was strictly observed. The building was divided by partitions and a grill and there was a different entrance in order for this rule to be strictly observed. The synagogue was set out in such a way that the Israelite as he entered turned his face towards Jerusalem.

At the centre was a platform, "bima", according to the ancient name or "almmeor". Those who were called up to read, went up by the side nearest their seat, and went down on the other side. There was a lectern on the bima known as a "migdal" or "wooden tower" from which were read the prescribed portions of the law and the prophets and from which sermons were delivered. The reader stood. The preacher sat.

The desk, lectern, chair or throne (churseja) or raised platform (pergula, from the Latin "pergula") rose in the middle of the bima opposite the ark. The latter was placed in the furthest part of the synagogue corresponding to the Holy of Holies in the temple, thus forming an essential part of the building.

It was called the "aron", (ark), the "tevah" or "tevutha" (ark like that in which Noah and Moses were saved from the water) or the "hechal" (little temple). It consisted of a chest or box in which the scrolls of the law were placed. The ark was mobile so that on some occasions, on a day of fasting or prayer for example, it could be carried into the street or into a square where the people were assembled. Sometimes there was a second chest for the scrolls of the prophets. Worn or damaged parchments of the law were kept in it.

Opposite the ark hung the "vilon" (velum, curtain), an imitation of the one before the holies. Above swung the "ner olam" or eternal light; near the ark was the eight-branched candlestick that was lit during the 8 days of the Feast of Dedication of the Temple.

In early times the crowd stood in the synagogue or sat on the floor. Later when worship services were made longer, chairs were installed. The congregation would sit looking towards the ark. The leaders of the synagogue, the priests, the distinguished Pharisees, all those who sought glory among men, claimed the front seats. They therefore sat with their back to the ark, looking towards the congregation.

There is a delicate question relating to a synagogue within the courtyard of the Temple of Jerusalem. People met in the chamber of hewn stones in the south-east corner of the

Left, the ruins of Samua. Below, those of a very ancient temple at Hazor (IXth century B.C.).

priest's courtyard. According to the testimony of contemporary writers, this room was also used for meetings of the High Sanhedrin. Their work was not confined to making legal decisions. Lectures were given and points of theology discussed. Therefore it might be that the word "synagogue" is in this respect used in its broadest sense. Similar buildings were in fact used in Palestine for these two purposes as well as being consecrated for celebrating the cult.

Part of the service consisted of a reading from the divine law, a reading of a pericope from the prophets and a sermon or talk. The liturgical element eventually took on considerable importance. This part consisted of prayers and the recitation of the blessing of Aaron: "the LORD bless thee and keep thee, the LORD make his face to shine upon thee and be gracious unto thee, the LORD lift up his countenance upon thee and give thee peace." Worship usually began with the Shema and was followed morning and evening by blessings pronounced by the Levites in the name of Jehovah.

The Shema and the benedictions were delivered from the reader's rostrum. The prayers which followed were said by the person presiding over the holy exercises after he had stood before the ark.

The prayers were directed or repeated aloud by a member of the congregation chosen for that purpose. The service ended with the priestly blessing pronounced by the descen-

dants of Aaron. When none of them was present, the group's delegate, as the leader of worship was called, repeated the words of the Scripture. When giving the blessing, the priests raised their hands level with their shoulders. In the Temple they raised them level with their forehead. The fingers of both hands were joined or separated in order to form five interstices. There was a mystical significance in this position of the fingers. It was forbidden by an old superstition to look at the hands of the priests, otherwise terrible punishments could strike the body of the offender. The Mishna however taught that any priest who had stains on his hands (or whose fingers were dirtied by paint) could not give a blessing, for fear of attracting the attention of the crowd. The body should be bent in prayer, but this position should not lead to lassitude such that the service seemed to have tired the congregation. One Rabbi said his system was to bend like the branch of a tree, and straighten up like a snake, starting with the head. With the exception of minors, any man chosen by the leaders of the synagogue could lead prayers. This only applies to the Shema. It was forbidden for anyone who was not properly dressed, for the blind who could not discern daylight, to pronounce the benedictions as such or the priestly blessing. If anyone introduced political ideas, or ideas considered as such, into his prayers, he was stopped immediately. If he had committed some impropriety, he was excommunicated for a week.

A service was held not only on the Sabbath and feast days but also on the second and fifth day of the week (Monday and Thursday),

The Holy Ark: ancient sculpture of Capernaum.

ult of the Samari-ıns: a priest raises ıe scrolls of the criptures. Right: nother aspect of ıe Samaritan cult: father makes a ıark above his oor with the blood f the lamb sacri-ed for the Pas-over.

Left, ancient religious lamps found in Jerusalem. Right, bench for the meetings before the synagogue of Capernaum. According to Christian tradition, Jesus taught on this very spot.

when the people from the country came up to the market, and the local Sanhedrin met to pass judgement on the cases of minor importance. In the week day services, three people were responsible for reading the Law; four the day of the new moon and during the intermediate days of a holy week; five during feasts and six on the Day of Atonement.

According to tradition, Moses had explained the Torah to Aaron, to his sons, to 70 elders and to the people, taking care that each of these categories had heard it four times. The Talmud (Talmud = doctrine, knowledge) tries to show that the set of traditional ordinances and the writings of the prophets and the hagiographs were communicated to Moses. It quotes as proof Exodus 24:12 "And the LORD said unto Moses, Come up to me into the mount, and be there; and I will give thee tables of stone, and a law, and commandments which I have written; that thou mayest teach them." The "tables of stone" according to one priest "are the ten commandments"; the word Torah means the written law in the Pentateuch: the "commandments" are the Mishna; "which I have written" relates to the prophets and the hagiographs. Hence all these things were communicated to Moses on Sinai.

Left: this summary sculpture of Beth Shean shows the chest of the Torah in a temple.

Jerusalem: detail of the Golden Gate. Right, corner tower of the city walls. "The City of David was regarded as the home of the children of Abraham."

10 - Death and its ceremonies

The scholars of the synagogue were careful, astute observers of the laws of health, and their rules were sometimes in advance of modern medicine. There are several indications that the art of healing, which had become so specialized in Egypt that every illness had its doctors, was also cultivated in Israel. The use of certain remedies, such as oil and vinegar for wounds, seems to have been very common among the mass of the people. Among the regular officers of the temple was a doctor specially for the priests who, inevitably since they celebrated the service barefooted, were frequently subject to disorders. The priests ordained that every town should have at least one doctor. He could perform operations when there was no surgeon available. Some of the rabbis themselves studied medicine. In theory at least, every doctor had to have a licence from them in order to practice. It was forbidden to seek help from a doctor who was a heretic, except in a case of dire necessity.

Although protectors of the art of Esculapus, the scholars of the synagogue were known to rail against this respected science. "Physician heal thyself" is really a Jewish proverb. "Do not live in a city whose first magistrate is a doctor" because he would busy himself more with public affairs and neglect his patients. "The best of doctors deserve Gehenna" (hell) for the unsatisfactory care he has given some, and negligence towards others.

They sometimes used sympathetic or magic formulae. Prescriptions ordered the use of simple bodies or compound salts. Vegetables were more used than minerals. Cold water compresses, natural or medicinal baths, and a special diet were carefully prescribed in some cases. Goats milk and barley soups were recommended in all illnesses causing a decline. Jewish surgeons seem to have known how to operate on eye cataracts.

The Children of Israel usually hoped to enjoy a long life. Death was regarded as punishment and the expiation of sins. When someone died before the age of fifty, he was said to have been cut off from amongst his people, at fifty-two, he died like Samuel the prophet; at sixty, death had been ordained by the hand of the celestial powers. Seventy was the end of an old man, eighty that of a strong man. The scholars compared a premature death to the fall of a fruit that had not reached maturity, or a flame snuffed out by a sudden draught. To leave the world without leaving a son behind, was to die like Joab. When a son survived his father, the latter slept in the sepulchre; thus it was for King David. If a man had finished his work, his death was seen as that of a just man who had gone to join his fathers. The tradition concluded, through a fantastic exegesis, from a simple phrase in verse 12 of Psalm 62 that there were 903 kinds of death. Quinsy was regarded as the worst and compared to tearing out a thread from a woollen cloth. The best death was likened to removing a hair from a bowl of milk, and it was called "death given by a kiss". This last expression derived from the following passages: Numbers 33: 38 and Deuteronomy 34: 5 where it is written respectively that they died "at the commandment of the LORD" and "according to the word of the

Tombs of the Prophets in the old Jewish cemetery of Jerusalem.

LORD". There were six people over whom the Angel of Death had no power: Abraham, Isaac and Jacob because they had seen their work finished before their last hour; Miriam, Aaron and Moses who died "in a kiss of God". Although premature death was punishment for sin, the just passed away because their task was to be given to other servants of Jehovah. Joshua was to undertake the task of Moses; Solomon that of David and so on. When the hour of death struck, everything could serve as an instrument of the Lord to inflict it. And the priests cried: "Oh Lord, all things serve thee, for the foot of man will carry him towards the aim that thou hast set him".

The way the dying man breathed his last sigh was also noted. If death was sudden, he had been swallowed up. If he died after one day's illness, it was a sign or reprobation: after two, of despair; after four, of reprimand; after five, natural death. If he expired with a gentle smile on his lips, eyes gazing upwards it was a good augur! If he looked down, and looked troubled, as if about to cry, or died looking towards the wall, these were all bad signs according to tradition.

If the sick man recovered his health, he had to perform acts of grace to the Lord. There was one superstition according to which if someone talked about his illness from the first day he worsened it, and prayer should be offered for him only on the second day.

Maimonides, the great scholar of Judaism, said that the duty of visiting the sick was the highest of all good works. The Talmud teaches that whoever visits the sick will save his soul from the fire of Gehenna. Thus one priest discusses the meaning of these words: "It is the Lord your God that you must follow", and he concludes that it is related to the imitation of divine acts mentioned in the Scriptures. God clothes the naked. Let us act in the same way. He visits the sick, consoles the afflicted and buries the dead, leaving us an example to follow. To encourage the Israelite, in this duty, he was reminded of the positive effects sympathy had on the patient, and was taught that whoever visited the sick took away the sixtieth part of their sufferings. Charity should not stop there. Burial of the dead was almost as pressing a duty as visiting the sick. When a funeral procession crossed the road, it was the duty of every onlooker to join the cortege if possible. The priests applied the following passages for the observation of this duty: Proverbs 14: 32 and 19: 7, and, regarding its negligence, 17: 5. The same thought was behind respect for the remains of the dead, and cemeteries were carefully preserved from any profanation. Even frivolous conversation was forbidden there.

Burial followed as close as possible on the moment of death. This was doubtless a measure of hygiene. Special reasons or respect for the relatives sometimes meant that burial was delayed for several days. The preparation of the burial of Christ mentioned in the New Testament, the anointing with scented oil, spices, the mixture of myrrh and aloes, all these customs are confirmed to the letter by the testimony of the priests of that time. At one time the cost

An ancient Jewish tomb.

of funerals was so high that they caused great difficulties for poor families who did not want in this respect to be inferior to their neighbours. There was extravagant expense not only for funerals but for the spices burnt near the tomb, the money and objects of value placed in the sepulchre, and even the sumptuous clothes in which the body was wrapped. Nothing less than the example of the priest Gamaliel was needed to introduce a very necessary reform. He ordered that his body should be buried in a simple linen gown. In recognition, a cup to bless his memory is drunk at funeral dinners. His grandson limited the clothing necessary for the dead man in his bier to a single garment. It was made with the cheapest linen material, and called the Tachrichin, the envelope, or shrouds. Furthermore, one priest ordered that he should not be buried in a white shroud for fear he should seem joyful, nor in a black garment for fear of seeming sad. He wanted to be wrapped in a red robe. Another asked to be dressed in a garment of white material to show he was not ashamed of his works. A third asked for his shoes, stockings and staff to be ready for the day of his resurrection.

The cemeteries were always outside the town. No road or canal could pass through them. No animal could graze there. We hear about public and private cemeteries. The latter were in gardens or grottos. It was the custom to visit the tombs, to weep or to pray. It was forbidden to eat, drink, or read, or even walk irreverently among the tombs. Cremation was forbidden as a pagan custom contrary to the spirit of the Scripture.

Tomb in the ancient cemetery of Tiberias. The friends of the deceased have brought stones here in the same way as Christians bring flowers to graves.

The body was carried on an open bier. The pall-bearers changed frequently in order to enable the largest possible number of those present to take part in such a worthy deed. Tombs placed in the fields were often decorated with monumental columns perpetuating the memory of the dead. Children less than one month old were carried by their mothers to the place of rest. Those less than one year old were carried on a bed or stretcher.

The order of the cortege was in perfect harmony with what we know of the customs of that time. If the event was taking place in Judaea, the mourners and musicians preceded the bier. In Galilee they followed it. First came the women, for in the words of an old Jewish saying, it is woman who brought death into the world, so she should lead the funeral procession. Behind the bier, in accordance with the law and the customs of the people, came a great multitude of people from the town.

At the tomb and on the road where the cortege made frequent stops, short speeches or a funeral oration were sometimes made. If the sepulchre was dug in a public cemetery, at least 1 ft. 6 ins. had to be left between the graves. Grottos or sepulchres cut into the rock had a hallway in which the bier was left and an inner chamber at a lower level than the first. According to the Talmud, these chambers were usually 6 feet long, 9 feet wide and 10 feet high. There were eight niches, three on each side of the entrance and two opposite, where bodies were placed horizontally. The largest sepulchres could take thirteen bodies. One large stone or a doorway barred the entrance to the tomb.

The rabbis make a distinction between Onen and Avel–the afflicted or suffering man and the broken man, wizened by the wind of trial, like a flower by the breath of the desert, that brings mourning. The first of these expressions applies only to the day of the funeral, the second to the days following it. Admittedly the Law of God prescribed mourning only for the first day, that of the death and the burial. The duration of the period following it was decided by the traditional ordinances. As long as the body was in the home, it was forbidden to eat, drink wine, tie phylacteries around the forehead or study. The necessary meals had to be prepared outside and if possible eaten away from the dead person. The first duty was to rend ones garments. This applied to one of several undergarments but not to the overgarments. The tear, on the front, had to be as long as the four fingers of one hand. When mourning a relative, it should never be closed; for other people it could be repaired after the fortieth day. As soon as the body had been removed from the house, all the chairs and beds were turned upside down and the afflicted person sat (except on the Sabbath and for only hour on Friday) on the ground or on a low set of steps. Here there were three distinctions. Deep mourning lasted 7 days. The first 3 days were called days of weeping. During this week of sadness it was forbidden, amongst other things, to wash, wear perfume, put on shoes, study or concern oneself with earthly matters. After this period, came a less strict period lastings 40 days. Children should mourn

Inscription on the tomb of a King of Judah.

their parents a whole year, and for 11 months (in order not to conclude that they needed to remain a whole year in purgatory) they had to recite the prayers for the dead. These however contained no intercession in favour of those who were no more.

The anniversary of the death was also celebrated. It was forbidden to mourn a man who had abandoned the faith of Judaism. On the contrary it was the rule to wear white garments on that occasion and make other shows of joy. We know that in exceptional circumstances the priests and High Priests were allowed to mourn their dead.

On returning from the ceremony, the friends and neighbours prepared for the family and mourners a meal of bread, hard-boiled eggs and lentils. It was said that this was round and vulgar food; round like life running ceaselessly towards the tomb. The food was served in earthenware dishes. Friends of the mourning family in turn took part in the funeral dinner when only ten glasses could be drunk, two before, five during, and three after the meal.

But after death what were the teachings regarding the judgement that followed? Who brought death to humanity?

The Talmud and the Targum tell us that heaven and hell were created before the world. There is a quote in the Targum of Jerusalem (on Genesis 3: 24) to prove it. It shows at the same time the current doctrine among the Jews. "Two thousand years before the universe was drawn from nothing, God created the Law, Gehenna and the Garden of Eden. He planted the Garden of Delight for the just, he wanted them to be able to savour the fruits and joys because in this life they had kept the commandments of the law. For the evil on the contrary he prepared Gehenna which is like a sharp sword with two cutting edges. He placed sparks of fire and burning coals to punish the wrong-doers in the world to come because even in this world they had not observed the precepts of his holy law. Is not this the tree of life? The man who observes it will live and dwell forever like the tree of life whose leaves never die." It was supposed that heaven and hell were near each other separated by a handsbreadth. There may be an allegory in this.

In conclusion take the following passage from the ancient Rabbinic writings "Rabbi Eliezer says : "Repent ye the day before your death." "Well", asked his disciples, "how can a man know the hour of his death?" "Repent today, then", replied the master, "for fear that you die tomorrow."

Opposite: sarcophagus of the 1st century one inscription of which says: "Salome, wife of Lazarus".

Left: A particularly impressive memory: The artificial hill "shaped like a breast" (according to Josephus) and the monumental fortress to which Herod gave the name Herodion. Place of refuge then tomb of the king.

Below, the candlestick of the Temple of Jerusalem carride to Rome after the triumph of Titus over the Jews (bas-relief of the Arch of Titus in Rome).

Crédits - Boyer : 54 - Giraudon : 142 - Gouvernement d'Israël : 12, 17, 24, 25, 27a, b, 28a, b, 29, 30a, b, 31, 34, 35, 40, 41b, 44, 46, 47, 53a, b, 55b, 65, 71, 73, 74, 91, 115, 122, 124, 125, 127, 143 - Mission de Ras Shamra : 63, 80a, b - Roger-Viollet : 2, 7, 8, 10, 11, 15, 18, 19b, 21, 22, 41a, 48, 49, 50, 56, 59, 62, 76a, b, 78, 85a, b, 86, 87, 88, 95, 96, 98, 102, 108, 109, 110, 111, 112, 116, 118, 119, 121, 129, 130, 131, 132, 133, 134, 139 - Walter : 19a, 23, 39, 43, 82, 92, 97, 120. Documents 55 a, 107 and cover p. 4 by courtesy André Parrot (« La Civilisation juive à l'époque du Christ » and « Abraham et son temps », Delachaux et Niestlé, publishers).

Printed in West-Germany